and

～ *william parker* ～

WILLIAM PARKER

～ *rebel without rights*

a novel based on fact by
JOHN ROSENBURG

The Millbrook Press ▪ Brookfield, Connecticut

Library of Congress Cataloging-in-Publication Data
Rosenburg, John M.
William Parker : rebel without rights / a novel based on fact by
John Rosenburg.
p.   cm.
Summary: William Parker, an escaped slave, defies the United
States government in the Christiana Riot of 1851, an event that
triggers the biggest treason trial in American history.
ISBN 1-56294-139-9
1. Parker, William—Juvenile fiction.   2. Riots—Pennsylvania—
Christiana—Juvenile fiction.   [1. Parker, William—Fiction.
2. Fugitive slaves—Fiction.   3. Slavery—Fiction.   4. Afro-
Americans—Fiction.   5. Riots—Pennsylvania—Christiana—Fiction.
6. Christiana (Pa.)—Fiction.]   I. Title.
PZ7.R71918sWi 1995   [Fic]—dc20   95-30209   CIP   AC

Photographs courtesy of The Bettmann Archive: pp. 25,
37, 60, 93, 126; The Library of Congress: pp. 35, 48 (both);
Moore Memorial Library, Christiana, Pa.: pp. 43, 85, 99,
104, 106, 139; Chester County Historical Society, West
Chester, Pa.: pp. 54, 73 (left), 112, 121; National Portrait
Gallery: p. 73 (right: NPG.80.21); John Rosenburg: p. 89;
North Wind Picture Archives: p. 97; UMI: p. 136.
Maps by Joe LeMonnier

This book is dedicated to a handful of warmhearted, generous individuals who have consistently supported and encouraged me over many years as I labored at the craft of writing, which, as every writer knows, is a lonely business that can often be more discouraging than rewarding.

These loyalists include: Ambrose "Herb" Linnen, A. Dennis Mollura, Raymond W. Smith and my wife, Rosemarie.

Anyone who has attempted to write a book about a historic event knows full well that it is an impossible task without help from many others in different fields. The writing of this manuscript proved to be no exception. Therefore, it is important to express my appreciation for the assistance of a wide range of individuals and organizations. They include the staffs of the Paoli Library, Chester County Library, Pennsylvania Historical Society of Philadelphia, the Lancaster County Historical Society, and the Chester County Historical Society — particularly photo archivist Pamela Powell — who gave freely and cheerfully of her time and provided some rare photos. Equally responsive was George Deeming, curator of the Pennsylvania Railroad Museum, located in Strasburg.

Also giving considerable help to this project were Ellen King and Barbara Crosson of the Moore Memorial Library in Christiana and Dr. Leroy T. Hopkins of Millersville University who critiqued the manuscript in its early stages.

Technical help was also given by Reference Librarian Charles B. Greifenstein of the historic Philadelphia College of Physicians. In addition, Patti Alexander also enthusiastically contributed an important piece of historical information that took a good deal of research.

On a different level and in a different vein, I am deeply indebted to Sara Sheppard-Landis, for her perceptive advice and wise counseling as the book progressed.

Naturally, I am grateful for the efforts of the many authors who have explored, researched, and written about the antebellum period, the workings of the Underground Railroad, and the life of William Parker. The basic document, of course, was Parker's autobiography. In addition, I was guided by Frederick Douglass's autobiography, and biographies of Lucretia Mott, Henry Clay, Daniel Webster, and John Calhoun.

Also most helpful were books by William Still *(The Underground Railroad)*, Jonathan Katz *(Resistance at Christiana)*, Margaret Bacon *(Rebellion at Christiana)*, James M. McPherson *(Battle Cry of Free-*

dom), Samuel Eliot Morison *(The Oxford History of the American People)* and Thomas P. Slaughter *(Bloody Dawn)*.

Other important sources included the transcript of the treason trial, accounts of the "Christiana Riot" by local residents (including one eyewitness story), and numerous news and magazine reports that appeared in the 1850s and 1860s.

Interviews with Mary Garrett and La Verne "Bud" Rettew, local historians, also contributed greatly to this work.

To all of the above go my heartfelt thanks.

John Rosenburg

The following text is based on William Parker's autobiography, on news stories, and on reports and books by Parker's Quaker friends, his enemies, and several historians. It is also based on the lengthy court record of the biggest treason trial in American history.

∽ *prologue* ∽

Compromise.

Compromise and the most divisive issue in American history will recede.

Compromise and a devastating civil war will be averted.

Compromise and the United States of America will be preserved.

So believed a shaky majority in Congress long before eruption of the bloodiest conflict the nation has ever known.

By then, of course, the arguments about slavery, pro and con, had reached an unprecedented crescendo, often spiked with violence. And by then eleven Southern states had already scheduled a convention to leave the Union and form a "confederacy."

Whether in the North or South, those who profited in some way from keeping four million blacks in bondage were obviously pro-slavery. For Southerners, as one South Carolina newspaper put it, slavery was "the great source of . . . prosperity, wealth and happiness."

Northerners, especially those in the textile mills supplied by Southern cotton, feared that if the fertile South were to secede it would take its trade East to Europe, rather than North. Mill owners and many of their blue-collar workers agreed it was best to support the South; if slaves were needed to pick cotton and preserve profits and jobs in the North, then slavery was fine.

Then there were the reactionaries who regarded those who would abolish slavery as "radicals"; people who were forever making trouble.

Slowly at first, then faster and faster, sentiment on all sides of the issue escalated.

Various religious groups—especially Quakers (and many Presbyterians)—grew more vocal and active in their opposition to slavery.

Anti-slavery newspapers and magazines sprang up through all the Northern states.

In several parts of the country—but especially in the North—there were violent clashes between slavery sympathizers and abolitionists. There were also numerous attacks against African Americans, some ending with lynchings.

Anti-slavery statements and writings by such well-known figures as Ralph Waldo Emerson, Henry David Thoreau, William Lloyd Garrison, and a former slave named Frederick Douglass, were published and widely circulated.

Northern opposition to slavery was hardened by more and more Southern forays into the Northern "free" states for the purpose of snatching former slaves from their homes and places of employment and by publicized advertisements like these:

Committed to jail, a man who calls himself John. He has a clog of iron on his right foot which will weigh four or five pounds.

Ran away, a Negro woman and two children. A few days before she went off, I burnt her with a hot iron on the left side of her face. I tried to make the letter M.

Still, the fact remained: slavery was legal where it existed. The United States Constitution said so. Even though the clause in the Constitution pertaining to runaways never used the word "slave," the intent was clear:

"No person held to service or labor" in one state and escaping to another could be "discharged from such service or labor" and must "be delivered on claim" to the slave owner.

The controversy over slavery steamed to a head in 1849, when California applied for statehood and the government acquired new western territory that would soon become Utah and New Mexico.

Should slavery be extended to these new areas?

Southern legislators declared that if the answer were no the South would leave the Union, as the balance of legislative power would be tipped and favor the North. To back up this threat, the Southerners planned to meet in Nashville, Tennessee, in July 1850 to do just that.

Some in the North answered: Good riddance! Let the South go and take slavery with it. There were others in both regions, however, who pleaded for a way to keep the Union together.

After extensive debate, Congress adopted a set of laws that became generally known as the Compromise of 1850. For the most part, these laws dealt with how slavery would be handled as the nation expanded westward into newly acquired territory.

For the South, however, the only positive feature of the Compromise was a tougher Fugitive Slave Act.

The new act heavily favored slave owners who laid claim to runaways and brought them before commissioners appointed by the federal government. Escapees, on the other hand, had virtually no rights under terms of the new law.

The burning question now was this: Could the new fugitive law be enforced? If it could, the Union might hold. If not, it appeared it would surely founder.

Twelve months after its adoption, the Compromise met its first major challenge in Christiana, Pennsylvania, a tiny hamlet in the southeastern corner of this supposedly "free" state.

More specifically, it encountered serious resistance at the home of an escaped slave. His name was William Parker.

～ *william parker* ～

*t*o his dwindling family and close friends, he was called William. To everyone else, he was known simply as Parker.

Physically, William Parker was big—big in every way. He was taller than most, stronger than most, more athletic than most.

Even his voice was big. When he spoke normally it boomed above all others. When he tried to lower his voice, it could still carry against a strong wind in an open field. And if he shouted, well, it was best not to be too close.

And while Parker had large, deep-set black eyes, a brilliant smile, a prominent nose, and higher-than-usual cheekbones, the most extraordinary part of his body was his hands—long, broad fingers; callused palms; wide, smooth backs; prominent knuckles.

Parker, a dark mulatto, was proud of his hands. They enabled him to do things others his age and older could not do. Especially when he closed them into fists.

As fists, his hands became potent weapons. Weapons he learned to use. Not because he wanted to. Because he was forced to.

It was late one Sunday afternoon in May of 1839 when Parker was about seventeen. The horse races for the day were over. And while the picnic tables were being cleared by their women, scores of white men from the plantations and farms of Maryland's Anne Arundel County jostled for position in a loose ring around Parker and another slave as they sat on tree stumps opposite each other in the grass infield of the racetrack, waiting.

Beyond the ring, in the trees and atop wagons and carriages, was another audience, black and mostly silent.

"Anybody else wanna bet against my nigger?" he heard Master Mack yell above the noise of the crowd. "Come on, come on, don't be bashful!"

Master Mack's gibes prompted a spate of raucous laughter and an exchange of banter and money, then a pistol shot. To a goading roar from the spectators, Parker and his bigger, older opponent, a black named Sam, rushed to meet each other in the center of the ring.

In this fight, like all others between slaves, there were no rules and no time-outs. The fight ended when one man was down and couldn't get up.

Parker won that day. In fact, he had never been beaten in the two years Master Mack matched him with others at horse races, farm sales, and county fairs.

After the battle, however, Parker reached a decision: he would no longer be used to fill the pockets of Master Mack and his friends with winnings from a fight that callously pitted one slave against another.

Nor would he be used in any other way. Not by Master Mack.

Not by anyone.

And from now on, he vowed silently, he would use his great fists and body to achieve but one goal: freedom from slavery.

*I*n truth, Parker had begun to dream of an escape to freedom years earlier. He'd been born into slavery on the plantation of Major William Brogden, not far from the site of his fearful battle with Sam.

Life on the farm was never easy. But it got worse after Major Brogden died, when his son—David McCullough Brogden—took over part of the property, calling it "Nearo."

Master Mack, as David Brogden was called, was a bad farmer, and the plantation began to lose money.

To make up for his losses, Master Mack began to sell his slaves to plantations in the deep South. They brought high prices because a machine called the cotton gin had been invented and dramatically increased the demand for slaves. (Until the gin came along, cotton had to be separated from seeds and hulls by hand. And right after the invention of the cotton gin, sugarcane became a major crop and this, too, brought a greater demand for field hands.)

While slave owners kept accurate birth records for their favorite dogs and horses, the births of children to slave parents were rarely noted. Unless, of course, these children came into the world at some important date or period: "planting time," Easter, "corn-husking time," Christmas, or New Year's Day.

Since Parker wasn't lucky enough to be born on any of these occasions, he never knew his birth date. Nor did he ever have a "birthday" to celebrate. He guessed, however, that he was about ten or eleven when he saw something for the first time that began to change his life.

It was a slave sale.

By then, his mother had died. And since he never knew his father, his only family included his grandmother, who cooked for the Brogdens, two brothers—Charles and John—his Aunt Rachel, her two children, and two uncles, Anthony and Dennis.

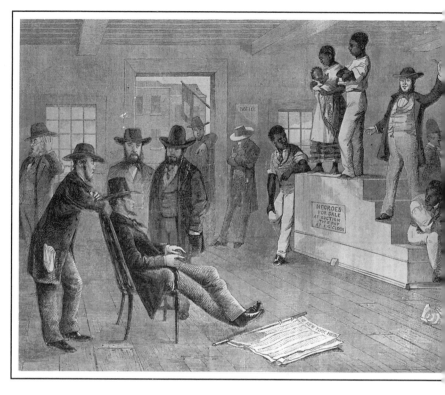

Slave auctions were common prior to the Civil War.
This artist's sketch shows a scene which is probably very
similar to what Parker witnessed as a child.

On the day of the sale, Parker and one of his friends, Levi Storax, a short, thin boy, ran into the woods, climbed a tall pine, and remained there until dark.

All the time they were in hiding, little Levi wept. Over and over again, Levi said, "They're gonna take my momma! They're gonna take my momma!"

But the slavers didn't take Levi's mother.

They took six others: Parker's younger brother, John, his two uncles, his Aunt Rachel, and her children.

Of course, Parker never saw them again.

*Y*oung and resilient, Parker recovered quickly from the bloody and brutal fight with Sam. And, while his body healed, his spirits rose. In fact, with each passing day, he grew more and more cheerful, even exuberant. This brought a warning from Charles.

"Listen, if you keep acting so happy, everybody'll know what you goin' to do," Charles whispered as they worked side by side planting corn.

"You're right!" Parker said, making a face as though he was about to weep, then laughing uproariously at his own silliness.

"I mean it!" Charles remonstrated. Then, more seriously, he asked in a low voice, "You still goin'?"

"Yep," Parker said firmly.

But before Parker was ready to flee Nearo, there was yet another slave sale at Master Mack's "Big House."

This time, it was the mother of Parker's next-best friend, Alexander Brown, who was sold.

As the slaver carted Alexander's mother off in a wagon, his sobbing friend, a big boy with long legs, ran helplessly behind. Finally, Alexander fell to the roadway. He was exhausted and could run no more.

An angry Parker helped Alexander back to the Quarter, the only home either of them had ever known.

Now Parker made up his mind: He would leave Nearo the next day. Even at the risk of capture and a beating with the rawhide.

*A*s eager as he was to leave Nearo, Parker hated the thought of going without Charles. But Charles, who at eighteen considered himself to be older and wiser than Parker, was still reluctant to consider so dangerous a move.

"But what have we got here?" Parker argued late that night. "We have no mother, no father, no home. And no life!"

There was a long silence as Charles weighed his brother's words. Finally, he spoke. "You're right," he said softly. Then, having made the decision, he suddenly became enthused. "Let's go! Let's go now!"

"No, no," Parker cautioned, putting a restraining hand on his smaller brother's arm. "Not now. In the mornin'."

"Why the mornin'? Let's go now while it's dark," Charles persisted.

"No. They's somethin' I gotta do first."

"What?" Charles wanted to know, not believing his ears.

"I gotta deal with Master Mack," Parker said, clenching and unclenching his hands.

"Whassat mean?" Charles asked.

It meant, Parker said, that he would face Master Mack in the morning and smash him to the ground!

"Then we'll run for the woods," Parker said.

Charles was aghast. "Smash Master Mack?" he asked. "What for?"

"I just have to!" Parker said. "He's gotta know how I feel about—about everything!"

Charles knew what he meant. But all he said was, "They's no need. He don't care how you feel. 'Sides, hittin' your Mastah means they hang you! So I say, let's go and let's go now!"

"No!" Parker said angrily. "Him and me is gonna have it out."

After a short silence, Charles said softly, "William Parker, sometimes I is sho you's crazy. Real crazy."

Maybe Charles was right, Parker thought at the time. After all, they had no money. They couldn't read or write. They had never lived off the plantation. And the only way they could travel was to walk.

Maybe the idea that they could make it all the way to the North was crazy.

But Parker refused to change his plan.

*t*he Quarter where Parker lived was a long, low, and narrow building. It looked like the chicken coop that stood only twenty yards away.

At each end there were open doors. And on each side, high up, there was a single window.

Those who lived in this building—in tiny rooms along each of the long walls—were either adults who were not married or children whose parents had been sold away.

Although it was raining when dawn broke, everyone was in the fields working. Everyone, that is, except Parker.

Parker was dressed that morning in the only clothes he owned: bib overalls, underwear, and a shirt. As he waited, he lay where he slept every night, on a thin pad stretched over bare ground.

Parker knew he would be missed. And when he was, he knew Master Mack would come for him.

But that's just the way he wanted it. A chance to meet Master Mack alone!

Ironically, it was Master Mack himself who prepared Parker for this critical moment in his young life. All the prize fights he'd arranged had given Parker great skill as a rough-and-tumble fighter. And they'd given him something else: confidence in himself, and courage.

As a result, Parker gave no thought to the possibility that he might be overpowered by Master Mack that fateful morning. Nor did he seem to care that, if he were, it would mean a severe beating, or the slave jail.

Or, worse yet, a rope around his neck.

*P*arker!"

Even before Master Mack's voice faded from the empty building, Parker was on his feet.

"Why aren't you at work?" Master Mack asked angrily.

Parker hesitated, then answered. "It's rainin' an' I'm tired."

Master Mack's eyes shot up in surprise. "Oh, is that so?" he asked mockingly.

Parker, poised and ready to defend himself, said nothing.

Master Mack, a tall man with a huge belly, picked up a long-handled ox goad that lay nearby. "We'll see about this," he said.

Raising the goad above his right shoulder with both hands, Master Mack shouted into Parker's face.

"You get to work, or I'll whip you good as sure as there's a God in heaven!"

When Parker refused to move, Master Mack swung the goad at his head. Parker ducked. Master Mack swung again. This time, Parker jumped forward, caught the stick in both hands, and grappled with his burly master.

With a sudden sharp twist and powerful jerk, Parker wrested the ox goad from Master Mack's hands. Now, he swung the goad at Master Mack, catching him across the left arm. Another blow and Master Mack was on the ground, writhing in pain and alternately cursing Parker and calling for help.

With his Master's cries ringing in his ears, Parker flew toward the fields.

Alerted by Master Mack's yells, Charles joined Parker in his race to a dark wood nearby.

The two boys hid until after dark. They then began the long, arduous walk to their first destination, faraway Baltimore.

"We're free!" Parker exulted as they moved along at a rapid clip.

"We ain't free 'till we shakes the dust of Maryland," Charles warned.

"Oh, they'll never catch us!" Parker said.

"Others said the same and look what happened."

"Not all, not all."

"Uh-huh," was Charles' panting reply as he tried to keep up with the longer legs of his brother.

But there was no stemming Parker's cheerful enthusiasm. "Trouble with you, Charles," he said, "you got no 'magination. Know what it's gonna be like up north? We gonna get jobs. We gonna get paid for them jobs. Our nights and our Sundays will be free. Best of all, we can do what we want with our money!"

"We ain't there yet," Charles cautioned.

Ignoring Charles, Parker went on, "Nobody watchin' us every minute. No more beatings. And you know what else?"

"What?"

"They can't sell us away!"

"Unless they come after us and catch us."

Abruptly, Parker stopped, faced Charles and grasped his brother by the shoulders. "But that ain't gonna happen," Parker said grimly, adding a vow, "I promise."

Little did he realize, however, how difficult and dangerous it would soon be to keep that promise.

*P*arker and Charles reached Baltimore two nights after leaving Nearo. They dared to move only when it was dark.

First they planned to comb the black community for someone to conceal them for the night. Then they hoped for a guide to where the Underground

Railroad began in Pennsylvania. The Railroad was actually a secret group of so-called "agents" and "station masters" who helped runaway slaves find their way to freedom, sometimes as far north as Canada.

Police patrols were everywhere, and since the clothes the brothers wore and their general appearance clearly marked them as farm boys, they knew they had to be very careful.

Maryland law gave slave owners and the police the right to seize escaped slaves at any time without a warrant. Those who helped locate or capture escapees could even expect a handsome reward.

Conversely, anyone in Maryland who helped a slave escape could be arrested and made to pay a heavy fine.

After dodging about the city for an hour, the boys came upon a brickyard. Though it was closed for business for the day, the gates to the yard were open.

"Come on!" said Parker, gripping Charles by the arm. "We're goin' in here."

"What for?" Charles grumbled wearily.

"Don't argue," Parker hissed. "Come on!"

Parker used his hands to scoop thick red dust from the ground and slap it all over Charles' clothes, face, and hands. All the while, Charles danced about, spluttering angrily, "Hey, hey!"

Then Parker repeated the process on himself.

"How do I look?" he asked Charles.

"Dirty," was Charles's sour response.

"Sure. Know why?"

" 'Cause you done gone crazy!"

"No," Parker grinned. " 'Cause now we're brick-yard workers and not farm boys."

The two moved boldly back to the streets. And no one took notice of them.

Parker's safe arrival in Baltimore, however, was only the first step toward what might or might not be freedom.

*b*y begging various black residents of Baltimore that first night in the city, Parker and Charles eventually found a family willing to take them in.

The family—a young husband and wife and two small children—were very kind to the boys. They fed them, allowed them to bathe, and fitted them out with fresh clothes.

For almost two weeks the boys remained hidden in the home of their new-found friends. During that period, local newspapers carried an advertisement describing them and offering a reward for their capture, or for information leading to it.

And all the while the police, Master Mack, his friends from neighboring plantations, and members

$200 Reward.

RANAWAY from the subscriber, on the night of Thursday, the 30th of Sepember,

FIVE NEGRO SLAVES,

To-wit : one Negro man, his wife, and three children.

The man is a black negro, full height, very erect, his face a little thin. He is about forty years of age, and calls himself *Washington Reed*, and is known by the name of Washington. He is probably well dressed, possibly takes with him an ivory headed cane, and is of good address. Several of his teeth are gone.

Mary, his wife, is about thirty years of age, a bright mulatto woman, and quite stout and strong.

The oldest of the children is a boy, of the name of FIELDING, twelve years of age, a dark mulatto, with heavy eyelids. He probably wore a new cloth cap.

MATILDA, the second child, is a girl, six years of age, rather a dark mulatto, but a bright and smart looking child.

MALCOLM, the youngest, is a boy, four years old, a lighter mulatto than the last, and about equally as bright. He probably also wore a cloth cap. If examined, he will be found to have a swelling at the navel.

Washington and Mary have lived at or near St. Louis, with the subscriber, for about 15 years.

It is supposed that they are making their way to Chicago, and that a white man accompanies them, that they will travel chiefly at night, and most probably in a covered wagon.

A reward of $150 will be paid for their apprehension, so that I can get them, if taken within one hundred miles of St. Louis, and $200 if taken beyond that, and secured so that I can get them, and other reasonable additional charges, if delivered to the subscriber, or to THOMAS ALLEN, Esq., at St. Louis, Mo. The above negroes, for the last few years, have been in possession of Thomas Allen, Esq., of St. Louis.

WM. RUSSELL.

ST. LOUIS, Oct. 1, 1847.

*When slaves ran away, their owners offered
rewards for their return in newspapers and
handbills, which were known as "broadsides".*

ᗰᗰ 35 ᗰᗰ

of his family roamed the streets of the city looking for them.

When the search seemed to be dying down, Parker and Charles swiftly left their hiding place. It was close to midnight when they struck out for Pennsylvania, just across the border from Maryland. Each boy carried a bundle of food. And each had memorized certain directions and landmarks as well as the names and locations of the few people who could help them along the way.

Here is the route Parker and his brother were told to take:

Go north to York, Pennsylvania. Then east to Wrightsville, a small town on the western bank of the Susquehanna River. Cross the river to reach Columbia on the east bank. One of the main "railheads" of the Underground Railroad is here. From this point, the railroad branches out in several directions. They could go as far north as they liked.

On the first leg of this journey, the boys walked along a railroad track, keeping a wary ear cocked for train whistles and an eye on the North Star to make sure they were headed in the right direction.

The second night out of Baltimore, they saw the lights of a small village in the distance.

"That oughta be Loganville," Parker said, peering through the darkness. "If it is, we've passed the border and York is only a few more miles ahead."

*Whole families were often helped by members
of the Underground Railroad.*

"Then we're free!" Charles shouted joyfully.

"If that's Loganville," Parker cautioned.

"It's Loganville, all right," a strange voice boomed out of the darkness.

The speaker sprang from a patch of woods bordering the track and planted himself squarely in front of Parker. Two more men moved stealthily out of the woods, blocking the boys on either side.

Obviously, they weren't free yet.

*t*he man in front of Parker had a large black beard and wore a floppy black hat. He carried a rolled up newspaper in his right hand.

"I guess you boys be the ones what run away from the Brogden place down in Maryland," the bearded man said.

"No, sir!" Parker replied.

"No need to lie," the same man said. "It's right here in the paper. We kind of figgered you'd come this way sooner or later."

"Yo makin' a mistake," Parker growled.

"No we ain't. So come on into town and don't make no trouble."

The man reached for Parker's arm. But Parker jumped aside, scooped up a heavy tree limb that lay beside the track, and swung at the bearded man.

CRACK!

Howling with pain and hugging his right arm to his side, the man dropped to the ground.

Parker swung again, landing a vicious blow on the back of the second man just as Charles landed a fist on the nose of the third.

In the next instant, the three men fled into the night, their bearded leader crying out that his arm was broken.

Knowing the trio would raise an alarm, Parker and his brother rushed toward York. Near the outskirts of the town they were hidden for the rest of the day by an elderly black farm couple.

Slave catchers were everywhere, they were told. They must cross the Susquehanna as quickly as possible since that broad and swiftly moving river was the real dividing line between North and South in that area.

As soon as it became dark, Parker and his brother hurried east along the railroad bed, again making sure the North Star was to their left. They walked in silence, too, having learned a lesson at Loganville.

Less than a mile from the bridge that spanned the river, however, Parker thought he heard voices. He and Charles stopped to listen. They were voices, sure enough, coming from behind and getting louder.

Parker pulled Charles off the road and into the underbrush. Dropping to the ground, they listened, hardly daring to breathe.

Soon, two men passed. One of them was clearly heard to say: "We gotta get to the bridge before they do."

Parker knew that voice. It belonged to Master Mack's brother-in-law!

And he knew the path to the east bank of the river would soon be blocked.

For several minutes, the two boys remained on the side of the road and, in low tones, discussed their situation.

Should they try to fight their way past the two men?

No, Parker decided. They had a contact in Wrightsville, a man named Robert Loney. They would try to find Loney, explain their dilemma, and seek his help.

Cautiously, they moved through the back streets of the little town until they found Loney's home.

A large man with a thick, gray beard, Loney had helped many runaways, but he never took one across the bridge.

"That's always watched," he explained. "There's a simpler way."

Without another word, Loney silently led the boys to the river bank several yards downwind of the bridge.

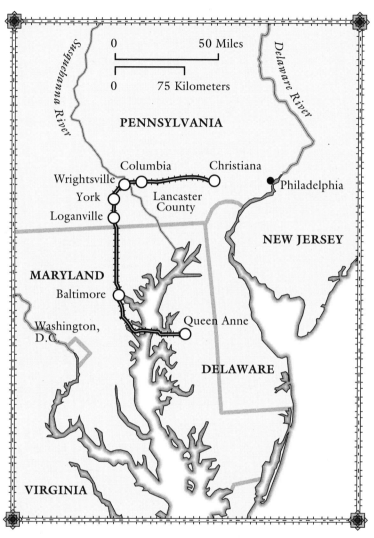

"I was born opposite Queen Anne, in Anne Arundel County,
in the state of Maryland. . . ." So began William Parker's
autobiography. His escape route from slavery took him to
Baltimore, a distance of 40 miles, then another 70 miles to
Wrightsville, Pennsylvania; all of it on foot.

There, the three slid quietly down the bank to the river's edge and boarded a small rowboat. Within thirty minutes the boys were in the Columbia home of a black member of the Underground Railroad, a widow who was quite old.

By noon of the next day, they were in eastern Lancaster County looking for work. They had to separate because jobs were scarce. But each of them found one—Charles as a farmhand and Parker as a construction worker for three dollars a month.

Thus, by the summer of 1839, Parker appeared to have left a life of slavery behind. But, he would soon learn, the "free" state he now lived in was not as free as he thought. Nor as safe.

*P*arker quickly became enraptured with Lancaster County, a large area in the southeastern corner of Pennsylvania.

It was, he soon learned, a land of numerous creeks and rivers, soft green hills, wide valleys, and exceptionally fertile soil. This, he decided, was where he would settle.

And since he liked to work with the land and watch things grow, he soon quit his construction job and went to work as a farmhand. For a time he drifted from job to job, but finally went to work for Levi Pownall, a Quaker farmer, in Christiana.

*A rear view of Parker's rented stone home
taken years after he left Christiana.*

A small stone house went with the job. It was located only a short distance from the large rambling home where Pownall lived with his wife, Sarah, and their four children.

Mr. Pownall was a big-boned, calm man with an angular, open face who rarely used two words where one would do. On the day he hired Parker he startled his new employee with this warning: "Not safe here for colored people."

"Why not?" Parker asked.

Mr. Pownall minced no words. "Underground Railroad runs through this county. Great hunting ground for slave owners and kidnappers."

Mr. Pownall explained that slave owners crossing the border from nearby Maryland had a legal right to seize their former slaves.

"And if they take them before a local judge with proper identification, there's nothing we can do about it," he said. "More and more, however, they ignore the legal niceties. Can't do anything about that, either."

"Why not?" an astonished Parker asked.

"Why not? Because they bust into homes in the middle of the night, hit victims over the head, tie 'em up, cart 'em off. Who's to stop them? The sheriff is twenty miles away."

When Parker asked how the slave owners were able to find runaways so easily in a strange state, he got a shocking answer.

"Informants," Mr. Pownall said sadly. "For a dollar, people will lead a slave owner right to where these poor individuals live." And, he added significantly, "Informants are not always white."

Worse than the slave owners, he went on, were the professional kidnappers.

"They live right among us, spy on us themselves, and pay others to spy on us," he said. "Take Red

Marsh. He's the leader of a gang of horse thieves, ex-convicts, and counterfeiters that makes its headquarters at a tavern in Gap, just a little west of here. We call 'em the Gap Gang."

When the Gap Gang identifies a runaway, it contacts the former owner, negotiates a price for the capture and delivery, then raids the victim's home, Mr. Pownall said.

"Unfortunately," he added, "they often kidnap black people who are legally free. Usually it doesn't matter to the slave owner. A slave is a slave."

*t*wo days after Parker's conversation with Levi Pownall, a black man was snatched from a farm only two miles away. Within the next three weeks, two more were taken from nearby farms.

For the following six weeks, however, all seemed peaceful.

But Parker knew the kidnappings could resume any time. And so, during that period he convinced members of the black community to come to his home after church on Sundays.

Generally, the get-together at Parker's was purely social. The men would pitch horseshoes, the women might make apple butter. Always there would be singing and often dancing.

But, little by little at these gatherings, Parker began to recruit several men to form a group to resist the kidnappers and slave owners whenever they might appear and again terrorize the black families in the area.

"We got to stick together for our own protection," he would tell each man he approached. "No one else is going to help us. Not the law. Not anyone."

"That could mean shootin' and killin'," one recruit commented.

"Yes," Parker said. "And it could mean your life or mine. But what choice do we have? Do we just let them take us? Or fight for what freedom we got?"

When he was sure of his men, the group was brought together for the first time. There were few formalities.

On a tattered Bible, each man was sworn to keep their identities secret. Then each voted for a leader. Parker was the unanimous choice. He was only eighteen.

In 1840, the forming of a black group of vigilantes was both a bold and a dangerous move.

a few days later, a boy on a galloping horse spread this word through Parker's neighborhood:

"William Dorsey's been captured and taken to the courthouse!"

Suddenly, the time had come for Parker's small band to act.

The courthouse, however, was surrounded by armed police who roughly shoved Parker and his men from its doors.

Fortunately, the windows were open on this hot summer day and much of the proceedings could be understood by those outside. After a brief hearing, the judge ruled that Dorsey was indeed the slave owner's property.

"We gotta get him loose," Parker told his followers.

"But the judge says Dorsey belongs to the slaver," someone protested.

"Hell with the judge," Parker cried. "If they take Dorsey South, you know what's gonna happen? His wife and four kids will be left here to starve!"

As Dorsey was led from the courthouse by police and the slave owner, Parker and his furious band surrounded him. The blacks pushed their way forward, trying to separate the prisoner from his captors.

The slaveholder drew a pistol and aimed it at one of Parker's men, William Hopkins.

"Get away, or I'll shoot," the slaveholder shouted.

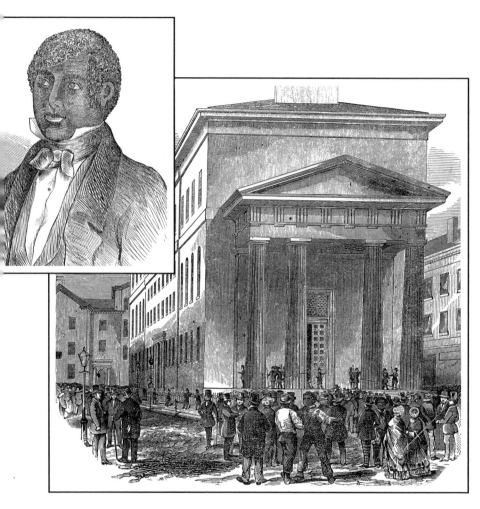

*In a case strikingly similar to Parker's effort to rescue
William Dorsey, a slave owner traveled from Georgia
to Boston to claim Thomas Sims as his property. A mob
of blacks and whites gathered outside the courthouse
and clamored for Sims's release, but he was returned to
his former master under heavy police guard. On his
return to Georgia, Sims was flogged in public.*

"Go ahead and shoot!" Hopkins responded.

Now the slaveholder aimed his pistol at Parker.

"If you and your rabble don't leave, I'll blow your black brains out," he cried.

Parker raised a fist, but someone from behind caught his arm. As Parker struggled to get his arm loose, a free-for-all erupted.

During the fight, which raged back and forth across the square in front of the courthouse, Dorsey was untied and set free. He was so confused, however, that he simply stood where he was.

All around Dorsey, Parker and the police and their deputies fought with clubs, sticks, and bricks. The battle moved across the road in front of the courthouse and swung back again. As it did, Parker's men got hold of Dorsey.

But just when it appeared he would be whisked to safety, reinforcements arrived and quickly overwhelmed the blacks. Dorsey was tied up again and hustled into the nearby jail.

During the melee, Parker was caught by the police several times. But each time, his enormous strength enabled him to break loose. Finally, the blacks were driven off.

Before nightfall, however, the black community and sympathetic whites in the area paid the slave owner for Dorsey's freedom.

It was only a partial victory for Parker's group, but a victory nonetheless.

*a*t daylight one morning not long after the Dorsey incident, a slave owner and two companions broke into the home of Moses Whitson and seized Elizabeth Jones, a slender black girl who lived there.

As they pulled her from the house, Whitson came running from the barn, his wife behind him. "Wait! Wait!" Whitson called.

The slave owner paused as he and his companions tried to put the struggling girl into their carriage. "Why should we wait?" the slave owner asked. "She's mine."

"No, I'm not," Elizabeth cried. "I don't know any of these men!"

"We can prove it," the slave owner said.

"Then take her to the courthouse and show your proof!" Mrs. Whitson said.

The discussion continued for several more minutes. Finally, the slave owner said, "This is a waste of time. Let's go!"

The Whitsons were Quakers and abolitionists. Their home was a station on the Underground Railroad. Since Quakers were opposed to violence, the Whitsons could do nothing to help Elizabeth.

Unbeknownst to the Whitsons and the kidnappers, however, Benjamin Whipper, a black man who worked for the Whitsons, saw what was happening from the hayloft of the barn. In minutes, he was on a horse and thundering to Parker's, sounding the alarm as he went: "Kidnappers! Kidnappers!"

While the slave owner had a good lead on Parker, he made the mistake of stopping at a tavern along the main road south.

When he took to the road again, Parker and seven others, all armed and mounted, were waiting in a small wood a short distance ahead. As the slave owner's carriage approached, they spurred their horses forward, forcing it to a halt.

A brief gun battle followed and two of Elizabeth's would-be captors were wounded. But Elizabeth was freed and she, Parker, and the rest of his band were unhurt.

Drawn by the sound of gunfire, a farmer named Henderson came on the scene and found the kidnappers nursing their wounds.

"What's going on?" Henderson wanted to know.

"We were taking our property back to Maryland," the slave owner answered, "when a bunch of niggers jumped us and nearly killed some of my men."

"Men coming after such property ought to be killed," Henderson said angrily.

Ignoring the remark, the kidnapper asked, "Do you know where we can find a doctor?"

"Oh, sure," Henderson responded. "There are plenty of doctors in the South."

The kidnappers drove off with Henderson's laughter ringing in their ears.

*b*y now Parker's home had become another station on the Underground Railroad. Whenever runaways arrived there, he would hide them overnight, then either find a home for them in the area the next day, or pass them to another station farther north.

Answering a timid knock at the door one night, Parker met fifteen-year-old Eliza Howard for the first time. She and her mother, Agnes Howard, had just come from Columbia, having been taken there by Robert Loney, the same man who helped Parker and Charles cross the Susquehanna many months earlier.

Eliza was a pretty girl with large black eyes and a trim figure. She was, he learned later, also strong-willed, but quick to laugh and burst into song.

While Agnes Howard slept, Eliza and Parker stayed awake and talked late into the night.

The next morning Parker took Eliza and her mother to a home in Christiana where they would be safe. But Eliza refused to stay there.

"I want to be with you," she told Parker.

"Good," Parker said, his heart leaping with joy.

Two weeks later, they were married. And between 1846 and 1849, three children were born to the couple—Marion, John, and Catherine.

During this period, Eliza's seventeen-year-old sister, Hannah Howard, also escaped from the South and moved in with them. And not long after her arrival, she met twenty-seven-year-old Alexander

Pinckney. Like Parker and Eliza they, too, fell in love and married. And because housing was so scarce in the area, the Pinckneys became part of the Parker household.

Far away in Washington, meanwhile, slavery, and all of its consequences, was being fiercely debated. The Union and the general public, it appeared, were about to be torn apart.

One man, however, came up with a proposal he believed would pacify the average citizen and even the most partisan member of Congress.

He was Henry Clay, a highly respected Senator from Kentucky.

*h*ailed in his youth as "Young Harry of the West" because of his fire and graciousness, by 1850 Henry Clay was old and sickly. Still, his mind was as agile as ever and his heart was strongly with his country.

"I go for honorable compromise whenever it can be made," he'd once said. "Life itself is but a compromise between death and life. . . . All legislation, all government, all society is formed upon the principle of mutual concession, politeness, comity, courtesy; upon these everything is based."

The compromise Clay offered that fateful year included: admitting California as a free state immedi-

Henry Clay, on the floor of the Senate, pleads for passage of the Compromise of 1850, a bill designed to keep the South from leaving the Union. Clay argued that the Compromise would "avoid the direful day when one part of the Union [could] speak of the other as an enemy."

ately; proceeding with the organization of Utah and New Mexico without reference to slavery—allowing the citizens of these areas to eventually make their own decision about slavery; ending the domestic slave trade in the District of Columbia (William Lloyd Garrison had said, "We are ashamed when we know that the manacled slave is driven to market by the very doors of our Capitol and sold like a beast in the very place where are assembled the representatives of a free and Christian people."); and adopting a tougher fugitive slave law.

Clay realized, however, that even with his great political influence he could never get his compromise plan accepted by Congress without help.

After all, the nation's legislators were equally divided on the issue of slavery. The House of Representatives, for example, had cast sixty-three ballots over a three-week period before it could agree on a Speaker a few months earlier.

As to the Senate, Clay would have to contend with the supporters of John C. Calhoun, the powerful Senator from South Carolina. It was Calhoun who urged the South to secede, arguing that the central government had too much power—so much that the states were losing their rights.

Even the president, a Southerner who owned slaves, and the vice president, a Northerner, failed to agree on how slavery should be treated in the new territories and states.

President Zachary "Rough and Ready" Taylor, a former General and the hero of the war with Mexico, was strongly opposed to Clay's "packaged" compromise plan and seemed inclined to veto it should he have the opportunity to do so. Taylor's only goal was to have California admitted immediately as a free state, with New Mexico to follow. Vice President Millard Fillmore, a lawyer from Buffalo, New York, appeared to be opposed to slavery.

One evening after dinner in his Washington home, Henry Clay called on Daniel Webster, the Senator from Massachusetts. Clay spent an hour with Webster, going over the details of his plan. At the conclusion, he was coughing badly and appeared exhausted. But he stayed another thirty minutes and the two discussed the political realities of Clay's proposal.

"You realize, of course, that the President may veto any legislation embracing your ideas," Webster said.

"Yes, that's a possibility," Clay said, nodding. "But he also believes in the need to preserve the Union, so he just might go along."

"And what about the Vice President?" Webster asked.

"I've talked to him," Clay said. "And if there's a tie—as there well could be—he would vote in favor of the Compromise."

When their talk was concluded, Webster said, "Your plan should be satisfactory to the North—and to the reasonable men of the South."

When he left Webster, Clay was a happy man.

Since the Southern convention called to split the Union was to take place in June, however, there was no time to lose.

On February 5, 1850, Clay rose in his Senate seat and pleaded his case for saving the Union. Weakened by a wracking cough, he needed the better part of two days to deliver his remarks.

In the debate that followed, Clay's proposal was immediately attacked by a Senator from Mississippi who said he was "grieved and mortified" that Clay, a Southerner, was not only inconsistent in his views but favored one section of the country over another.

Clay denied any inconsistency, saying pointedly, "On the question of slavery, I shall go to my grave believing it is an evil, a social and political evil."

"I intend, so help me God," he added, "to propose a plan of doing equal, impartial justice to the North and South. I consider us all as one family, all as friends, all as brethren. I consider us all as united in one common destiny and those efforts that I shall continue to employ will be to keep us together as one family, in concord and harmony; and above all to avoid that direful day when one part of the Union can speak of the other as an enemy."

But the Senator from Mississippi persisted, saying Clay had turned his back on the South. "The persecuted South has looked to him as one of her safest, most influential and distinguished sons [but now] he has given the North all the trump cards in the pack."

Getting to his feet once more, the weary Clay responded acidly: "I know whence I came, and I know my duty, and I am ready to submit to any responsibility which belongs to me as a Senator from a slaveholding state . . . I know no South, no North, no East, no West, to which I owe my allegiance. My allegiance is to this Union and to my own state; but if gentlemen suppose they can exact from me any acknowledgment of allegiance to any ideal or future contemplated confederacy of the South, I here declare that I own no allegiance to it; nor will I, for one, come under any such allegiance. . . ."

It was, as one newspaper put it, a statement of "towering grandeur" and one that made all those who advocated a Southern confederacy "tremble."

But this was only the opening salvo. Now, it was up to Webster.

*A*lmost three weeks after Henry Clay's appeal for unity, Daniel Webster wrote to a friend that he was "nearly broken down with labor and anxiety."

"I know not how to meet the present emergency," he wrote, "or with what weapons to beat down the Northern and Southern follies, now raging in equal extremes."

But the following week, he decided to deliver a speech in support of Clay.

On March 3, however, a packed Senate first heard from Calhoun, once described as the "moral and intellectual colossus" of his age. Calhoun, too ill to deliver his own remarks, asked James Mason of Virginia to read his speech.

As expected, Calhoun made many of his usual points. Compromise, he said, could only be achieved among those with equal power. The South was no longer equal to the North. He said the North and South should separate peacefully unless the South was given equal rights in the new territories, the North returned to the South the fugitive slaves it was protecting, and put an end to "agitation of the slave question."

Four days later, it was Webster's turn.

To most Americans, Webster was the greatest orator of his time. Many claimed he was the greatest in history—world history, some embroidered.

So it's not surprising that when Webster announced in advance on March 7, 1850, that he would speak out on the most important issue of the day, America cocked an attentive and nervous ear toward the nation's capital.

Daniel Webster's famous and historical "Seventh of March" speech is credited with convincing Congress to vote for passage of the Compromise of 1850.

In Washington itself, according to the *New York Daily Times,* crowds of men and women "besieged every door of the Senate chamber" to hear what Webster had to say.

The vice president convened the Senate at noon with a single rap of his ivory mallet. By then, according to the *Times,* "there was not a single unoccupied spot in that chamber, above, or below, or in any avenue leading to it where Mr. Webster's voice could not be heard."

But Webster was not the first to speak. The floor was given to Senator Walker of Wisconsin so he could finish a speech started the day before.

To applause and a roar of appreciation from the tense spectators, Senator Walker rose and said, "Mr. President, this vast audience has not assembled to hear me; and there is but one man, in my opinion, who can assemble such an audience. They expect to hear him, and I feel it to be my duty, as well as my pleasure, to give the floor to the Senator from Massachusetts."

Webster, with his mane of coarse black hair, black eyes, black bushy eyebrows, and craggy features looked, many said, "like a sleepy lion."

But when Webster delivered what became forever known as his "Seventh of March Speech," there was nothing sleepy about him, nor his audience.

*L*ike Henry Clay, Webster was well along in years, but as the *Times* noted in its report, he had lost none of his eloquence:

". . . The speech came on, as the Mississippi rolls from its fountains, increasing in depth and width till it terminates in the ocean . . ."

Wearing, as always, a buff vest, a blue dress coat adorned with brass buttons, and a gleaming white ascot, Webster began:

"Mr. President, I wish to speak today, not as a Massachusetts man, nor as a Northern man, but as an American and a member of the Senate of the United States.

"It is not to be denied that we live in the midst of strong agitations and are surrounded by very considerable danger to our institutions and government. The imprisoned winds are let loose. The East, the North and the stormy South combine to throw the whole sea in commotion, to toss its billows to the skies, and disclose its profoundest depths."

After a pause, he thundered:

"I speak today for the preservation of the Union!"

And then, for all who were divided on the issue of slavery—and especially the warring Congressmen of the North and South—he placed himself squarely behind Clay's plan.

California already had a constitution that contained "an express prohibition of slavery, or involuntary servitude," he pointed out.

As to extending slavery to the new territories, ". . . wherever there is substantive good to be done, wherever there is a foot of land to be prevented from becoming slave territory, I am ready to assert the principle of the exclusion of slavery."

Turning to the thorniest issue of all—the proposed fugitive slave law—Webster tried to reason with those in the North certain to oppose it.

"We must view things as they are," he said. "Slavery does exist in the United States. It did exist . . . before the adoption of [the] Constitution and at that time."

The fact was, the clause that established the original fugitive slave law was favored by virtually every state when the Constitution was adopted in 1787.

The "clear historical truth" was that the Convention "meant to leave slavery in the states as they found it, entirely under the authority and control of the States themselves."

"Every member of every Northern legislature is bound by oath, like every other officer in the country, to support the Constitution of the United States; and the article of the Constitution which says to these states that they shall deliver up fugitives from service is as binding in honor and conscience as any other article . . . In that respect the South . . . is right and the North is wrong."

As to the proposed law—which would give slave owners pursuing escaped slaves more power than ever, his position was clear. He would support the law ". . . to the fullest extent."

As his three-hour address—given with scarcely a glance at his notes—drew to a close, he castigated those who favored secession, or splitting of the Union.

"Secession!" he cried. "Peaceable secession! Sir, your eyes and mine are never destined to see that miracle. . . . Is the great Constitution under which we live, covering this whole country, is it to be thawed and melted away by secession, as the snows on the mountain melt under the influence of a vernal sun, disappear almost unobserved and run off? No sir! No sir! . . . I see as plainly as I see the sun in heaven what that disruption itself must produce; I see that it must produce a war!"

His voice expanding with emotion, Webster's oratory rose to new heights at his conclusion:

"And now, Mr. President, instead of speaking of the possibility or utility of secession, instead of dwelling on those caverns of darkness, instead of groping with those ideas so full of all that is horrid and horrible, let us come into the light of day; let us cherish those hopes which belong to us; let us devote ourselves to those great objects that are fit for our consideration and our action; let us raise our conceptions to the magnitude and importance of the duties that devolve upon us; let our comprehension be as broad as the country for which we act, our aspirations as high as its certain destiny; let us not be pygmies in a case that calls for men!"

While several Southern Senators spoke against the Compromise on the usual grounds, a Northern voice brought out a new and different view.

Senator William H. Seward of New York warned that while Congress had the constitutional right to extend slavery westward, ". . . There is a higher law than the constitution which regulates our authority over the domain. . . ."

He said the proposed Fugitive Slave Act was more dangerous than any anti-slavery law. "All measures which fortify slavery or extend it," he said, "tend to the consummation of violence; all that check its extension and abate its strength, tend to its peaceful extirpation."

At the conclusion of the debate, the Southern convention, called to take the South out of the Union, failed.

And, after the sudden death of Zachary Taylor and the elevation of Millard Fillmore to the presidency, the Compromise of 1850 became law.

*L*ate in the summer of 1851, just before the new set of laws crafted by Clay and Webster went into effect, the Gap Gang spotted an advertisement offering a reward for a runaway slave said to be the property of a woman living in Elkton, Maryland.

"Ain't that John Williams?" Perry "Red" Marsh asked, thrusting the paper at his cronies as they stood around the bar at Clemson's Tavern.

"Sure looks like him," answered one member of the Gang.

"That's him, all right!" said another. "Lives on Marsh Chamberlain's place."

"Yeah," another chimed in sourly, "And awful damned close to Parker's."

"Let's not worry about Parker yet," Marsh said. "Let's find out how much this old lady is willing to pay for Williams."

"Right," laughed another. "Money talks!"

After an exchange of correspondence, the Gang agreed to return Williams to the Maryland woman for two hundred dollars.

Late one night, knowing Chamberlain was away, the Gap Gang surrounded his house. Peering through the windows, they saw Williams on a chair near the stove.

The only other person in the room was Thomas Pennington, Chamberlain's elderly father-in-law. His daughter, Rachel Chamberlain, was presumed to be somewhere on the second floor.

"Perfect," Perry Marsh whispered to his men. "Let's go!"

At the signal, the gang members broke into the house and shoved Pennington roughly aside as Marsh put a pistol to Williams's head.

"Come along, nigger, and don't make no fuss," Marsh said threateningly.

"I ain't goin' anywhere!" Williams said, jumping up from his chair and knocking Marsh's gun aside. As Pennington fled to the upper floor to join his daughter, the six gang members piled on Williams and beat him into unconsciousness.

They then dragged him out the door, tied him to the back of a horse, and rode off, their victim in tow.

Rachel Chamberlain and her father had watched the fight through a heat vent in the floor of an upstairs bedroom. When Rachel was sure the Gap Gang was gone, she rushed out of the house toward Parker's, calling his name.

"William! William!" she cried.

Parker, who was at home chatting with his brother-in-law Alexander Pinckney and a friend named Samuel Thompson, heard Rachel and dashed out of the house to meet her.

Hearing her story, Parker called to Pinckney, "Alex, you and me will take two of Chamberlain's horses and go after them! Sam, go get some of the other boys and follow us."

Parker and Pinckney reached the Maryland border about dawn. But the kidnappers had eluded them.

Later that week, Parker told Pinckney, "I heard the Gang got nothin' for poor Williams."

"Why not?" Pinckney asked.

"They fractured his skull and beat him up so bad, the woman who advertised him wouldn't pay them."

News of Williams's fate spread quickly through the county, arousing the anger of several abolitionists. Six of them gathered at the home of Lindley Coates, a Quaker.

"Somehow, we have got to bring an end to the lawless and ruthless raids of the Gap Gang on the blacks of this area," Coates said.

"Let's have the Gang arrested and taken to court," one farmer suggested.

"Good idea." said another. "Rachel Chamberlain and her father saw the whole thing. They could be our witnesses."

Convinced they could finally put the Gap Gang behind bars, two farmers, Dr. John Cain and Samuel Whitson, were appointed to consult a lawyer.

The lawyer advised, however, that nothing could be done.

"Why not?" Dr. Cain wanted to know.

"Because Williams was returned to his legal master."

"But he was beaten and abducted and we've got witnesses," Whitson protested.

"I'll admit his return was not strictly according to law," the lawyer said. "But I don't think you can find a jury that will vote against the Gang. And you know the reasons as well as I."

Reluctantly, the farmers dropped the matter. But the Gap Gang had big ears. Barns belonging to Whitson and Coates, both agents of the Underground Railroad, mysteriously burned to the ground the following week.

That same week, word seeped out of Clemson's Tavern that the Gap Gang was going to "get Parker."

$\mathcal{E}$dward Gorsuch, a Maryland plantation owner, was known as a man who treated his slaves kindly, setting them free when they became twenty-eight years of age, then offering them jobs.

Gorsuch was also a religious man. It was said that he was so religious that every Sunday he attended one church in the morning, another in the afternoon, and sometimes a third in the evening.

When a letter from Lancaster County, Pennsylvania, reached Gorsuch's home near Baltimore, his reaction was predictable: the Lord had spoken!

But the letter was not merely an answer to his prayers; it was a response to an advertisement he had placed in several newspapers.

The advertisement had given physical descriptions of four black men, saying they were thieves and escaped slaves. And it gave their names as Nelson Ford, Noah Buley, and George and Joshua Hammond. As in all ads of this nature, a hefty reward was offered for information leading to the capture and arrest of the four.

Although the handwriting and the grammar were poor, the letter replying to the ad was abundantly clear.

"Respected Friend," it said, "I have the required information of four men that is within Two miles of each other."

In the letter, dated August 28, 1851, the writer not only gave the Maryland slave owner detailed information about the escapees, he offered this intriguing plan to capture them:

". . . now the best Way is for you to come as A hunter disguised about two days ahead of your son and let him come By way of Philadelphia and get the deputy Marshal John Nagle I think is his name. tell him the situation and he can get a force of the right kind it will take twelve so they can divide and take them ALL within half an hour, signed: very respectfully thy friend . . . William Padgett."

Ordinarily, Padgett made his living by traveling around Lancaster County repairing clocks and watches. As he did so he befriended newly arrived black people to learn what he could about them.

Black, but so light-skinned he could pass for white, Padgett was a member of the dread Gap Gang.

Spurred to action by Padgett's letter, Edward Gorsuch fired off a reply.

"When do we meet and where?" Gorsuch asked.

Within a week, a rendezvous had been arranged. During that period, Gorsuch had organized a posse that included his son, Dickinson Gorsuch; a nephew, Joshua Gorsuch; a cousin, Dr. Thomas Pearce; and two neighbors who were also slave owners.

On the night of September 7, 1851, Gorsuch got together with his group to make final plans.

"I'm taking the express to Philadelphia tomorrow," he said. "The rest of you meet me there at the Philadelphia Hotel the day after tomorrow. We'll then take a train to Lancaster County."

"You'll have a marshal?" Dr. Pearce asked.

"I expect to, yes," came the reply.

On his arrival in Philadelphia, Gorsuch went immediately to the office of one of the newly appointed fugitive slave commissioners.

"I want four warrants and a marshal to enforce them," Gorsuch demanded.

The commissioner, eager to show how efficient he was in his new job, quickly complied with the request.

"Just describe your boys on these papers," he said, "and we'll put things in motion."

The deputy marshal assigned to the case was Henry H. Kline, a tall, black-bearded man with a high-pitched voice who was slightly deaf. Kline was directed to head up the posse and make the necessary arrests.

"I'll leave for Lancaster tomorrow and meet you there the day after," Kline told Gorsuch.

What Gorsuch and Kline didn't know was that the commissioner's office was being watched by a secret committee of black abolitionists headed by William Still. No sooner did Gorsuch obtain his four warrants than a messenger was off to Christiana with all the details.

*b*y the time the Compromise of 1850 became law, Parker was about twenty-eight. While he still couldn't read or write, he managed to keep up with events in the world beyond Christiana.

On Sundays after church, or evenings after work, he often called on local Quaker families and other educated whites to discuss current affairs. These friends would frequently read pertinent magazine and newspaper articles to him.

He also attended community meetings where slavery and other matters were discussed. On one occasion he visited adjoining Chester County to hear anti-slavery lectures by fiery William Lloyd Garrison and eloquent Frederick Douglass, a former slave.

To his surprise, he discovered he had met Douglass after one of the fights Master Mack had staged at a farm sale. "Back then," he told Eliza, "I knew him as Frederick Bailey."

While he was much impressed by the eloquence of Garrison, it was Douglass who moved him most.

"I have never listened to the words from the lips of mortal man which were more acceptable to me," Parker told Eliza.

Parker eagerly shared what he learned with the men, women, and children who inevitably became his followers.

There would also be serious talk about their status as citizens and the controversy about slavery. And

Parker said he once listened outside the open window of a meeting hall to the fiery anti-slavery speeches of William Lloyd Garrison and former slave Frederick Douglass.

always, Parker, with his big booming voice and flashing black eyes, would pound home the message that they were free and had the right to remain free.

As a result, Parker was not surprised on that Wednesday in September of 1851 to find a crowd gathered in his yard when he came home from plowing Levi Pownall's fields.

"Kidnappers comin'!" someone yelled as soon as he was seen coming through the orchard to the north of the house.

"Posse with a slaver and a marshal," another called to him.

As the excited group discussed the situation, a two-wheeled cart behind a fast horse careened down the lane and stopped at the house.

Levi Pownall's wife, Sarah, dropped the reins, climbed down from the cart and quickly approached Parker. The broad face beneath her bonnet showed great concern.

"You heard," Parker said simply.

"Yes," she said. "And I trust thee will not resist."

"I will do what I have to do," Parker said.

"William, listen to me," she said seriously. "Slave owners have the full force of the law—Federal law— behind them. If you resist, there will bloodshed!"

"If the law treated us the same as whites, I would not fight," Parker said. "But the laws are not written for us. And we are not bound to obey them. You have a country and should obey the law. But we have no country."

"Thou should really leave for Canada," Mrs. Pownall said.

"No."

With a sigh of regret, Mrs. Pownall went back to her cart and drove off.

That night, seven people settled down in Parker's house: the Pinckneys, the Parkers, Abraham Johnson, and two of Gorsuch's former slaves.

Somewhere between the headquarters of the Gap Gang and Christiana around four in the morning of Thursday, September 11, the Gorsuch party met the man who was to lead them to Gorsuch's slaves.

He appeared to be white, but was masked, so it was difficult to tell.

"You didn't bring as many as I thought," the masked man said.

"What difference does that make?" Edward Gorsuch asked gruffly.

"Well, if we had another marshal and another six men, we could get them all tonight," came the reply.

"So what do you suggest?" Gorsuch asked.

"Me-thinks it's best to make one raid at a time," the masked man replied.

"Fine," Gorsuch said. "Let's get going."

After a long ride, the masked man stopped the posse at a stream that burbled through the valley in which Parker lived. Pointing into the darkness, he said, "There's where two of 'em are, in a little house."

"How do you know?" Kline asked.

"I know." was the response.

"Can't see very much," Gorsuch complained.

"It's only a few yards up the lane," the masked man said. "Now, how about my pay?"

"Can't it wait 'til after the capture?" Dickinson Gorsuch asked. "After all, we can't be sure our boys are there."

"We been watchin' 'em. They're there. Now, gimme my money, or the deal is off." With that the masked man drew a gun and added, "Two shots and your niggers will be gone like a pair of scared rabbits."

"No, no," Edward Gorsuch said. "We'll give you your money."

After the money was counted out, their guide said, "I'll be in touch with you about the other two tomorrow."

The posse now hunkered down on the bank of the stream, nibbling on cheese and crackers while they waited for daylight.

As daylight came, the Parker house was obscured by a ground fog. Soon it began to lift and the house became clear.

With Marshal Kline leading, the Gorsuch party moved quietly forward. As they did so, a black man came out of the house and started down the path that led to Long Lane.

It was Joshua Kite, one of Gorsuch's slaves. (Like almost all escapees, Kite had changed his name.) Convinced the posse wasn't coming, Kite had decided to go to work. When he spotted the Gorsuch group, however, he turned and ran back into the house yelling, "Kidnappers! Kidnappers!"

•

*J*oshua Kite flew through the front door of Parker's house and up to the floor above, where the other six were gathered at the front windows to see the posse that had come to capture the Gorsuch runaways.

Unfortunately, Kite left the front door open.

"If you boys come down and go home with me, there'll be no trouble," Gorsuch called up the stairs.

"If you take one of us, you take us all over our dead bodies," was Parker's reply.

Several pieces of wood flew out of an upstairs window and struck the members of the posse still in the yard below.

Inside, Kline and Edward Gorsuch were at the foot of the stairs. Parker stared down at them from the top as Kline put a foot on the lower step.

"Take another step and I'll break your neck," Parker thundered.

Kline stopped. "I am a United States Marshal," he squeaked, losing some control of his voice.

"I don't care who you are," Parker said, "you'd better not try to come up!"

Alexander Pinckney tugged at Parker's arm. "Let's give up," he whispered.

"Have you gone crazy?" Parker said out of the side of his mouth as he looked down the stairwell.

"No," Pinckney answered. "But what's the use of fighting?"

"I never took you for a coward, Alex."

"I'm not a coward," Pinckney pleaded. "But why get killed? They'll take us anyway."

"No!" Parker hissed. "We're not giving up to any slaver!"

"You hear that, Alex!" Eliza said, shaking a fist under the nose of her brother-in-law.

Now Gorsuch moved ahead of Kline. "Come on," he urged. "Let's go up and take them. I want my property and the law is in my favor."

Kline didn't move, but Gorsuch started up the stairs, prompting Parker to warn him. "You can come up," said Parker, "but you can't go down again. Once you're up here, you're mine."

A five-pronged fish spear and an ax flew down the stairs, barely missing Kline and Gorsuch.

Kline then read the warrant to Parker. When he finished, he said, "You understand what that means, Parker? It means me and my deputies are commanded to take you dead or alive. So you might as well give up!"

Parker didn't answer. Encouraged, Kline said, "I'm coming."

"Come on," Parker responded almost gleefully.

But instead of advancing, Kline retreated.

Calling up the stairs, Gorsuch said, "I want my property and I want it now!"

"Men are not property," was Parker's reply.

In a loud voice, Kline now called to his posse, "Fetch some straw from the barn. We'll burn 'em up!"

"Burn us up, you coward, and be welcome!" Parker roared. "Before I surrender, you'll see my ashes scattered to the winds."

Hearing Kline's threat, Eliza picked up a horn, leaned out the window and blew it with all her might. This well-known call to all who heard it meant: "Help! Help! Help!"

Realizing the sound of the horn might bring reinforcements for Parker's little band, Kline called to his men, "Shoot that bitch!"

Immediately, a volley of shots rang out. But Eliza, her head safely behind the thick stone walls around the window, kept blowing and blowing and blowing the horn.

After a brief rest to catch her breath, she led the group in singing the chorus of a slave hymn:

Leader what do you say
About the judgment day?
I will die on the field of battle,
Die on the field of battle,
Die on the field of battle,
Glory in my soul!

*A*s the standoff continued, Gorsuch and Kline retreated to the yard.

Parker leaned out an upstairs window with a pistol in his hand.

"I want my property and I will have it," Gorsuch shouted angrily.

"I haven't got your property," Parker said.

Gorsuch, pointing to Parker, said to Kline, "Shoot that damned nigger!"

Kline promptly raised his pistol and fired at Parker. He missed, but broke the windowpane above Parker's head.

Infuriated, Parker raised his gun and aimed at Gorsuch's chest. He squeezed the trigger, but Pinckney struck his arm and the bullet sailed over Gorsuch's shoulder.

Now Gorsuch asked Parker in a severe tone, "Does not the Bible say 'Servants obey thy masters'?"

"Does not the same Bible say 'Give unto your servants that which is just and equal'?" Parker responded.

Gorsuch was undeterred. " 'Let all who are under the yoke as slaves regard their own masters as worthy of honor so that the name of God and our doctrine may not be spoken against.' "

"But where do you see it in Scripture that a man should traffic in his brother's blood?" asked Parker.

"Do you call a nigger my brother?" cried Gorsuch.

"Yes!" Parker thundered.

Marshal Kline now tried another ploy to get Parker and his friends to give up. Handing a note to one of the posse, he loudly announced, "I'm asking the sheriff at Lancaster to send a hundred men!"

Parker was not impressed. "Bring five hundred!" he called to Kline. "You will need all of them to take us alive."

Although Kline had faked the call for help, a large group of white men suddenly came out of the woods and moved toward the house.

Under authority of the Fugitive Slave Law, Kline quickly deputized all as his special constables.

The Pinckneys now begged Parker to give up. "I'm not afraid," Pinckney said, "but what's the sense of just five of us trying to fight all of them?"

"Be still, both of you!" Eliza cried, raising a fist.

"I'm going down," Alexander Pinckney said.

"No!" Eliza said. "You stay!"

"If you try to go down, I'll shoot you," Parker warned.

Pinckney stayed where he was. But he had good reason to be worried. The group Kline had deputized included the vicious Gap Gang.

Clearly, they saw their enrollment by Kline as the opportunity they had been waiting for. Now they could end Parker's interference with their activities once and for all.

But the Gap Gang would be the least of Parker's concerns.

•

*J*ust as Marshal Kline finished deputizing members of the Gap Gang and others, two more white men appeared.

One of them, a tall, gaunt man, was riding a sorrel gelding with a blaze face. The other, a burly man with a thick, gray beard, was on foot.

The rider was Castner Hanway, a newcomer to Parker's neighborhood and the owner of a grist mill. Behind him was Elijah Lewis, a Quaker and local storekeeper.

"Hey, you two!" Kline called out. "Come 'ere."

When the two men hung back, Kline hurried toward them. He explained that he was a deputy U.S. Marshal.

"Now here are my warrants for these niggers in the house," he said. "And I want to deputize you two to help me get 'em under arrest."

"You're not deputizing me," said Lewis, immediately turning away from Parker's yard.

"Nor me," Hanway said, walking his horse behind Lewis.

Kline followed the two men, arguing that the law made it mandatory that they be deputized when called on to do so by a federal marshal.

Just then, there was a burst of cheering from the house. From every direction, blacks armed with corn cutters, scythes, axes, and guns could be seen converging on Parker's home. And in the front ranks were Noah Buley and Josh Hammond, two more of Gorsuch's former slaves.

Unarmed, Parker came down the stairs and hurried into the front yard a few feet from the Gorsuches. Eliza and the others moved in behind him.

Suddenly, some twenty blacks and twenty whites were face to face, tensing for battle.

A voice from behind the group of whites called out: "Mr. Gorsuch! Mr. Gorsuch! We better leave, sir." It was Kline.

'I'm not budging without my property!" Gorsuch replied.

Coming closer, Kline addressed Parker. "We don't want any bloodshed, Parker. If you'll withdraw your men, I'll withdraw mine."

"We're staying put," was Parker's grim reply.

Kline turned and ran toward Hanway and Lewis.

"You sirs!" he called to the still retreating pair. "Don't let them niggers start anything."

Hanway turned in his saddle to speak to Kline. As he did so, he saw a black man raise his gun. Alarmed at the prospect of a shootout, Hanway cried out, "Don't shoot! For God's sake, don't shoot!"

The black man lowered the gun and Hanway and Lewis started off again. Kline followed them, still arguing. "If anything happens to Mr. Gorsuch's slaves, I'll hold you two responsible," he blustered in his high squeaky voice.

When Lewis and Hanway ignored him, Kline turned and called out to his group, "You men, withdraw! Withdraw, I say!"

The two groups remained locked in place. Silently, they watched Gorsuch and Parker as the two men, standing face to face, continued to argue.

"I'll ask you one more time," Gorsuch said. "Give me my property."

"And I'll tell you one more time," Parker came back, "those men are not your property!"

Dickinson Gorsuch, standing next to his father with a pistol in each hand, interrupted.

"Father, why take all this from a nigger?"

Parker looked coldly at the young man and said, "You repeat that remark and you'll lose your teeth."

Dickinson Gorsuch was seriously wounded in the so-called Christiana Riot. His father, Edward Gorsuch, was killed.

Angered, the younger Gorsuch raised both pistols and fired. The shots went through Parker's hat, creasing his skull in two places.

As the pistols exploded, Parker charged young Gorsuch and knocked one gun from his hand. Dropping the other gun, Gorsuch ran for the orchard.

Alexander Pinckney apparently had a change of heart about the wisdom of resisting, for he raised a double-barreled gun and fired once, knocking the slave owner's son to the ground. When young Gorsuch got up and continued running, Pinckney fired again and Gorsuch fell a second time.

At the sound of the first shot, the battle erupted between the Gorsuch and Parker forces. Fierce blows were struck by both sides amidst a wild burst of gunfire.

Believing the blacks were getting the upper hand, the whites retreated, ending the fight almost as quickly as it began.

Both sides had some minor wounds, but Dickinson Gorsuch lay bleeding in the orchard.

His father, Edward Gorsuch, was on the ground at Parker's feet.

He was dead.

*P*arker was covering Edward Gorsuch's body with a sheet when Levi Pownall arrived at the scene seated on the jouncing driver's bench of an open wagon drawn by a galloping horse.

On reaching Parker, Mr. Pownall lifted his chin toward the sheeted body.

"Who's that?"

"Slaver named Edward Gorsuch," Parker replied.

Something next to Gorsuch's body caught Pownall's attention. It was Gorsuch's hat. Picking it up, Pownall plucked a piece of folded white paper from inside the crown.

"What's that?" Parker inquired.

"Letter," Pownall said. He started to hand the letter to Parker, but suddenly remembered Parker couldn't read. "Padgett to Gorsuch."

"Padgett, the clock man?"

Pownall nodded. "Looks like he guided the posse."

"Well, that answers a lot of questions," Parker said darkly.

"Anybody else hurt?" Pownall asked.

"Some minor wounds," Parker said. But then, pointing to the figure of Dickinson Gorsuch in the orchard, he added, "But that one could be serious."

Pownall strode quickly to young Gorsuch, Parker following.

After bending down to examine the slave owner's son, Pownall straightened up and said, "Take him to my house."

The two men carefully loaded Gorsuch into the bed of Pownall's wagon. "Won't live," Pownall told Parker with a sad shake of the head as he was about to drive off. "You and thy friends had best leave and hide."

Parker and his followers needed no urging. Within an hour, all involved in the fight were gone, scattered in different directions like dry leaves before a still wind.

It was a wise move.

*T*he next morning, the streets and walks of Christiana were clogged with humanity, horses, mules, and two- and four-wheeled conveyances of every type. People from the whole area, it seemed, had gathered in the town to hear what officials had to say about the death of Edward Gorsuch.

Gorsuch's body had been taken to Fred Zercher's hotel, where it was to be examined by coroners.

On completion of the examination, a coroners' jury was selected and met behind closed doors in the hotel dining room. In less than thirty minutes, the following verdict was read to the crowd jamming the area around the hotel:

"On the morning of September 11th, 1851, the neighborhood in the vicinity of Brick Mill was thrown into excitement by the deceased and others in company with him, making an attack upon a family of colored persons for the purpose of arresting some fugitive slaves, as they alleged. Many of the colored people of the neighborhood collected and there was considerable firing of guns and other fire-arms by both parties. Upon the arrival of some of the neighbors at that place after the riot subsided, they found the deceased lying on his back, or right side, dead.

"Upon post mortem examination upon the body of the deceased, made by Drs. Patterson and Martin, in our presence, we believe he came to his

Once known as Zercher's Hotel, this building was where the body of Edward Gorsuch was taken, the coroner's verdict announced, and the preliminary court hearings held.

death by gunshot wounds that he received in the above mentioned riot, caused by some person or persons unknown."

Undaunted by the verdict, Marshal Kline circulated in the crowd to find witnesses to what he termed "a dastardly murder."

One of the first he approached was a small, timid black man named Harvey Scott.

"Hey you!" Kline said, grabbing Scott by the scruff of the neck. "You were at the shooting yesterday, weren't you?"

"No, sir!" Scott cried out.

"Don't lie to me!" Kline yelled, shaking Scott roughly. "You were there, say so!"

Thinking a positive answer might mean he could get away from Kline, Scott answered, "Y-y-es sir."

"That's better," Kline said, releasing Scott. "Now, if you help me I'll see you don't go to jail. Understand?"

"Yes, sir."

"What's your name?"

"Harvey Scott."

"All right, Harvey," Kline said in a kinder tone, "now what I need you to do is give me the name of every nigger who was at Parker's."

As he interrogated Scott, a man with flaming red hair and a red beard tapped Kline on the shoulder. It was Perry Marsh, the leader of the Gap Gang. Bill Baer, another member of the Gang, was at Marsh's elbow.

"We got some more names for ya, if you want 'em." Marsh said. "But we can't be witnesses."

Marsh and Baer, eager to get rid of some of their enemies, fed Kline several names of blacks, many of whom were not at the scene of the battle. They also agreed to show Kline where all of those named lived and suggested how they could be captured.

That afternoon, Kline appeared before a local judge and charged fifteen blacks and Caster Hanway and Elijah Lewis with the "murder of Edward Gorsuch." (Dickinson Gorsuch was still alive.)

The principal witnesses were Kline and Harvey Scott.

A short time later, Lancaster County District Attorney John L. Thompson arrived in Christiana and issued warrants for those accused by Kline.

Hearing that they were wanted, Hanway and Lewis surrendered to the local sheriff fifteen minutes after their warrants were issued.

Fearing they would be attacked, the sheriff decided to lock them up for their own protection. As they were being led away, they were confronted by Kline.

"You lily-livered scoundrels," he yelled. "Yesterday, when I pleaded for my life like a dog and begged you not to let the blacks fire on us, you turned around and told them to do so!"

Hanway remained silent, apparently too stunned by the accusation to comment.

"What you are saying is a lie," Lewis said calmly. "And I will remind you that before the shooting started, you ran into the woods so you'd be safe."

With Hanway and Lewis in jail, the sheriff called for volunteers to hunt for the rest of the suspects.

More than a hundred whites responded, including a crew of tough Irish immigrants who were laying railroad tracks in Christiana. They were willing to help the sheriff because they'd been told that blacks posed a serious threat to their jobs. (In the North, in fact, there had been five or six riots in various cities, as whites attacked blacks when they competed for jobs.)

The sheriff deputized forty-three of the volunteers, all of whom seemed bent on avenging the "murder" of a white man by "rioting blacks."

*d*uring the next twenty-four hours, rumors that a bloody, black insurrection had erupted in Christiana swept through southeastern Pennsylvania and areas far beyond.

Word of this inflammatory situation was telegraphed to Washington, prompting an emergency meeting in the White House among Millard Fillmore, the nation's thirteenth president, Secretary of State Daniel Webster and Attorney General John C. Crittenden, a former Senator of Kentucky and a follower of Henry Clay.

"Mr. President, we've got to move swiftly on this," Webster said, as they gathered in the president's office.

Fillmore, a tall, handsome man with a large oval face, big brown eyes and neatly combed gray hair, said, "People tell me that a hundred times a day, Mr. Webster."

Millard Fillmore, the nation's thirteenth president, signed the infamous Fugitive Slave Act into law. A year later he made the decision to crack down on Parker and his followers for defying the law, calling their act treason.

Flipping his coattails up, the president seated himself at his desk, clearly irritated at being summoned from a formal private dinner for a foreign dignitary. "So what are the facts?"

Attorney General Crittenden took a deep breath and began again. "A group of coloreds in a place called Christiana, Pennsylvania—just outside of Philadelphia—resisted arrest by one of our marshals and several deputies."

"Why?" Fillmore asked.

"The marshal had warrants for four runaway slaves. He attempted to return the slaves to their master, a man named Gorsuch. A fight broke out between the coloreds protecting the runaways and the marshal and his deputies. Gorsuch was killed and his son critically wounded."

Now Webster spoke. "In other words, we have a group of people who defied the Fugitive Slave Act, a group of people who thumbed their noses at the government of the United States. Now, we have an agitated South waiting to see if this government intends to enforce the law. A South ready—nay, eager!—to secede if we falter for one moment in our sworn duty!"

After a short silence, the president said, "I have to admit, we cannot expect the South to live up to its Constitutional obligations if those in the North refuse to live up to theirs."

"Well put, Mr. President," Webster said, relieved.

"So what do you suggest?"

"I suggest we round up the culprits immediately, arrest them, and hold them for trial," Crittenden said.

"On what charge?"

"Treason, sir," came the reply.

"Treason?"

"Sir, to prosecute only on the basis that the suspects defied the Act would not be severe enough—

would not satisfy the South. We've got to convince the South we view this matter very seriously."

"Yes, yes, I see that," Fillmore replied. "But treason? I hope we have sufficient grounds for such a charge."

"Conspiring to make war on the United States in the person of a U.S. Marshal is certainly sufficient grounds," he was assured.

"Maybe," Fillmore said.

Webster, tired of the wrangling, said bluntly, "It's that or risk a civil war."

"Go ahead then," the president said wearily.

"*A*rrest all those who defied, or conspired to defy, the United States, as represented by Marshal Kline. Suspects to be charged with treason."

These were the orders flashed from the White House to John Ashmead, the U.S. Attorney for Pennsylvania.

Since treason is the nation's highest crime and punishable by death, the president, it was clear, hoped to convince the South and advocates of slavery that the government fully intended to quash all opposition to the Fugitive Slave Act.

Within a few hours, Ashmead and a U.S. commissioner arrived in Christiana from Philadelphia, bringing with them forty-three U.S. marshals and forty-four U.S. Marines from the Philadelphia Navy Yard.

The commissioner promptly held a hearing that again featured Kline and Scott as the chief witnesses. It lasted two days before being postponed and moved to Philadelphia.

During that period, the federal and local authorities put together a force of more than two hundred men, including members of the Gap Gang.

In groups of eight and ten, the "deputies," mounted on horses or driving wagons and carriages, fanned out in different directions. From daylight to dark, the posses swept through Lancaster and Chester Counties in a relentless search for Parker and all others accused by Kline.

The manhunt created an unprecedented reign of terror. The deputized representatives of law and order, which included several drunks, invaded the homes of both blacks and whites without warning, destroyed furnishings, stole valuables and horses, torched barns, and roughly handled suspects.

An elderly white man plowing a field near Christiana, for example, suddenly found himself surrounded by horsemen. Two dismounted and rushed toward him. One grabbed him by the throat while the other pinned his arms behind his back.

"You Joseph Scarlett?"

With his wind cut off, the farmer could only nod.

The hunt for those responsible for Gorsuch's death resulted in what one newspaper called a "reign of terror."

"You was at Parker's weren't you?"

Despite protests, Scarlett was bound and thrown into a wagon. This scene was repeated many times during the course of the roundup.

As a Lancaster newspaper reported, "Gangs of armed ruffians from Maryland, assisted by the lowest ruffians this region of Pennsylvania can furnish, were prowling the County and arresting indiscriminately all colored persons they met . . ."

When the search ended, all females caught (including young girls) were released. Among them, ironically, were Eliza Parker and her sister, Hannah Pinckney.

Twenty-four blacks and three whites were held, however, and promptly shipped in a cattle car to Philadelphia, where they were jailed. The whites were Hanway, Lewis, and Joseph Scarlett.

Scarlett had not been at Parker's, but had ridden through the Christiana neighborhood to warn everyone that kidnappers had surrounded Parker's house.

When the Philadelphia hearings ended, forty-one people, including six whites, were indicted. (Never before or since in American history have so many been charged with treason at one time.)

Among those named (in absentia) was the man authorities wanted most—William Parker. As yet, he had not been captured, or even reported as having been seen.

White defendants Castner Hanway, Elijah Lewis, and Joseph Scarlett, shortly after the treason trial ended.

*V*irtually all points of view about the Christiana clash were reflected in the nation's newspapers as word of what was variously described as an "uprising," "riot," "rebellion," or "insurrection" spread across the country.

The most slanted views, of course, were in the anti- and pro-slavery press.

William Lloyd Garrison's *Liberator,* for example, said Parker and his followers were "fully justified in what they did by the Declaration of Independence."

"That Gorsuch should have been shot down like a dog seems to us to be the most natural thing in the world," another publication declared.

A South Carolina newspaper, on the other hand, revived a call for secession by asking its readers to "throw off the accursed yoke that is galling us. . . ."

But there were different views. A Rochester, New York, newspaper noted that there had been an upsurge in the sale of firearms to blacks "with the avowed intention" of using them against anyone called on to execute the Fugitive Slave law.

"Let the Negroes buy as many revolvers as they please," the paper commented, "but they may rest assured that the first one that is used by them against our citizens will be the signal for the extermination of the whole Negro race. . . ."

A Boston paper declared, ". . . all the rights and claims and apologies are on the fugitive's side. He only did what any white man would be applauded for doing."

Yet, the paper asserted that armed resistance to the law was "bad," adding, "The offenders will have to suffer."

Several newspapers blamed the abolitionists for the riot. The Philadelphia *Bulletin,* for example, noted that the "melancholy tragedy of Christiana" had "established in blood the dangerous character of the modern abolitionists."

Another Philadelphia paper, *The Sun,* said the blacks accused of "the unwarrantable outrage" at Christiana were but "tools," then added, "The men who are really chargeable with treason against the United States Government . . . are unquestionably white, with hearts black enough to incite them [the blacks] to commit any crime. . . ."

Still another paper insisted the abolitionists were "the real if not the chief instigators" of the riot.

Horace Greeley's powerful New York *Tribune* walked a middle line, saying first that the "divine law of Nature" supported Parker and his friends, but then added, "whatever be the absolute right in this case, it is plain that the blacks fell into lamentable error. They ought to have followed the advice of their friends [the Quakers] and escaped from the country."

In Florida, a report pondering Gorsuch's death asked, "Are such assassinations to be repeated?" and concluded, "If so, the sword of Civil War is already unsheathed."

The New York *Independent* blamed the Christiana "affray" on the Compromise of 1850. "The framers of this law counted upon the utter degradation of the negro race — their want of manliness and heroism — to render feasible its execution," the paper said ". . . They anticipated no resistance from a race cowed down by centuries of oppression, and trained to servility. In this, however, they were mistaken. They are beginning to discover that men, however abject, who have feasted upon liberty, soon learn to prize it and are ready to defend it."

The Lancaster *Examiner and Herald,* however, called Gorsuch's death "one of the most horrid murders ever perpetuated in this county or state."

Still, within a week of the riot, said the Philadelphia *Ledger,* "the matter was looked on in a far different light. Thousands were soon aroused to sympathy who had hitherto been dormant. . . . Hundreds visited the prisoners in their cells to greet, cheer and offer them aid and counsel. . . ."

A Lancaster newspaper noted that there was a "fervent heat" of indignation aimed "not so much at the Negroes as at those who instigated them to the deed."

"We have long foreseen such an issue; God grant that the future has nothing worse in store growing out of the same cause . . . but we have an ominous premonition that this is not the end, but only the beginning."

The article carried the prophetic headline:

CIVIL WAR—
THE FIRST BLOW STRUCK.

*W*ith Parker still at large, the treason trial began in Philadelphia on November 24, 1851, in the very building where both the Declaration of Independence and the Constitution were signed—Independence Hall.

Six lawyers represented the government, three of them from Maryland. For the defense, there were three lawyers, including Thaddeus Stevens, a U.S. Congressman and well-known abolitionist.

The prosecution decided to try each case separately. They began with Castner Hanway. Since he was white, a conviction would tell the South that the government was serious about punishing those who defied the Fugitive Slave Act. A conviction of Hanway also meant a conviction of the other defendants as the evidence against each was identical.

The formal charge against Hanway, read at his arraignment, ran to several hundred words. A key section declared:

Thaddeus Stevens, famed U.S. Congressman and abolitionist attorney, was one of three members of the defense team.

"You Castner Hanway, with a great multitude of persons . . . to the number of one hundred persons and upwards, armed and arrayed in a warlike manner, that is to say, with guns, swords and other warlike weapons being then and there unlawfully and traitorously assembled, did traitorously assemble and combine against the said United States and with force and arms, wickedly and traitorously oppose and prevent, by means of intimidation and violence, the execution of the said law of the United States."

"How say you, Castner Hanway, are you guilty or not guilty?" the clerk of the court asked after the charges were read.

"Not guilty," Hanway replied.

"How will you be tried?"

"By God and my country," Hanway answered solemnly.

*f*ederal Attorney John Ashmead launched the government's case, saying Hanway was charged with "a crime of a highly aggravated character; in its nature, the most serious that can be perpetrated against a human government."

"It is technically called high treason," he told the jury of twelve men. "It consists in this country only in levying war against the United States, and in ad-hering to their enemies, by giving them aid and comfort."

To the most critical point he said, ". . . any individual who joined a group that used force to prevent execution of a Federal law—such as the Fugitive Slave Act—is guilty of treason."

Ashmead outlined the following "basic facts" about the case for the jury: "First—that so soon as Hanway appeared—the negroes in Parker's home appeared evidently encouraged, and gave a shout of

John W. Ashmead led the prosecution's team of six lawyers that sought to appease the South by convicting three whites and thirty-five blacks of treason.

satisfaction; when before that they appeared discouraged and asked for time.

"Second—that before the firing commenced, Kline had given orders to his party to retreat, and they were actually engaged in the retreat when the attack was made.

"Third—that Edward Gorsuch, who was killed, had no weapon of any kind in his hands, and was therefore cruelly, wantonly and unnecessarily wounded by the defendant and his associates while carrying out their combined conspiracy to resist, oppose and render inoperative and void the acts of Congress referred to in the indictment."

Ashmead said he would prove the defendant guilty for the following reasons: Hanway and others had "forcibly" prevented the execution of the Fugitive Slave Act. In doing so, Hanway "did wickedly and traitorously levy war against the United States." He and others had rescued Gorsuch's escaped slaves. He had prepared and distributed literature that urged people to resist the Fugitive Slave Act.

To back up his charges, Ashmead called a number of witnesses, the most important being Marshal Kline and his black supporter, Harvey Scott.

Kline portrayed Hanway as the leader of the riot, claiming the blacks had cheered when he arrived at Parker's house. He said it was Hanway who had ordered Parker and his little band to open fire on the Gorsuch party.

When Scott took the stand, he repeated all he had said in Christiana.

*d*efense attorney Theodore Cuyler said the case against Hanway was "the most absurd and groundless prosecution ever instituted in this or any other court of justice. He is an innocent man, most unjustly charged with this high offense," Cuyler said of Hanway.

Cuyler noted that "on the borders of Lancaster County there resides a band of miscreants, who are well known to the records of the penitentiary in this state. They are professional kidnappers," he said. "These men, by a series of lawless and diabolical out-rages, have invaded the peace of Chester Valley— bringing dread to every household, and a general sense of insecurity to every home.

"In consequence of this, there was a general feel-ing of indignation against these professional dealers in human flesh, not against lawful authority."

In winding up his opening to the jury, Cuyler said mockingly of the charges, "Did you hear it? That three harmless and non-resisting Quakers, and eight and thirty wretched, miserable, penniless negroes, armed with corn-cutters, clubs and a few muskets and headed by a miller, in a felt hat, without a coat, without arms and mounted on a sorrel nag, levied war against the United States?

"Blessed be to God that our Union has survived the shock."

*t*he defense team realized almost from the outset of the trial that if the defendants were to go free they must somehow discredit the two main witnesses—Marshal Kline and Harvey Scott.

This pair alone, they reasoned, identified the forty-one defendants as participants in the fight that caused Edward Gorsuch's death.

A second objective was to show that the blacks at Parker's were justified in trying to protect themselves.

Defense attorney Cuyler began by calling Rachel Chamberlain's father to the stand and asked him to describe what happened when the Gap Gang entered the Chamberlain home.

"I was standing between the door and the black man," Thomas Pennington said. "He was sitting behind the stove with his boots and hat off. They passed right by me to him and presented a pistol to his head and they told him they would blow his brains out if he made any resistance."

At another point in his testimony, Pennington was asked if he recognized the kidnappers.

"I know one of the persons that came in," he answered. "He had the pistol."

"And who was he?" Cuyler asked.

"Perry Marsh," came the answer.

"The leader of the Gap Gang?"

"Yes."

Then came Elijah Lewis, who directly contradicted Kline's testimony that Hanway had incited the blacks and caused them to attack the whites.

"The fact is," Lewis said, "that Mr. Hanway begged the coloreds *not* to shoot."

"And did you not have a conversation with Dr. Pearce, one of Gorsuch's party, a few moments later?" Cuyler asked.

"Yes."

"And what did he say?"

"He told me that Hanway had saved his life, that the gun Hanway saw was aimed at him."

Lewis also testified that Kline had left the scene of the battle long before the shooting started and could not have seen or heard Hanway urge the blacks to launch an attack.

After several more witnesses, the defense began to attack Kline's character.

William D. Kelley was the first witness called in this regard.

"Do you know Mr. Henry H. Kline?"

"I do," came the answer.

"Do you know his general character?"

"I believe I do."

"Do you know his general character for truth and veracity?"

"I have heard it much spoken of."

"What is it?"

"Very bad."

Twenty-four other witnesses called by the defense gave virtually the same answers to the same questions.

*a*fter a long day in court, the three defense attorneys—Theodore Cuyler, James Cooper and Thaddeus Stevens—were having dinner in the all-male dining room of a private club near Independence Hall when several women swept by a protesting headwaiter and approached their table.

The lawyers could tell from the plain dresses and bonnets that the women were Quakers. The obvious leader was a small woman with deep gray eyes.

She was Lucretia Mott, one of the nation's leading crusaders for women's rights. A Philadelphian, she was also a vigorous abolitionist who often appeared on the same platform as Frederick Douglass.

"I'm Lucretia Mott," she said on reaching the lawyers. "My friends and I are members of the Female Anti-Slavery Society."

After the headwaiter was waved away and further introductions made, Thaddeus Stevens said, "How can we help you?"

"We want to visit your clients," the fifty-seven-year-old Mrs. Mott said promptly.

"Really?" the astonished Stevens said. "Why, may I ask?"

"Mr. Stevens," Mrs. Mott said in a scolding tone, "those colored men are still in the summer clothes they wore in the fields when they were arrested. It's winter. And if we don't get them something warmer, they'll die in those damp, unheated cells."

The actions of Lucretia Mott, president of the
Female Anti-Slavery Society, and her friends gave
a dramatic twist to the treason trial.

"Are you saying you want to furnish them winter clothes?" Cuyler asked. "All of them?"

"Of course!" came the tart reply. "We'll make them. And not with cotton or wool produced by slaves, mind you. But we can't do a thing until we get measurements."

"But, you'd have to go to the prison to do that!" Cooper said.

"Naturally. That's why we're here. To get your cooperation."

"Well, I don't know—" Cooper began.

"You've got an admirable idea!" Stevens broke in. "We'll make the arrangements immediately."

"Thank you, Mr. Stevens," Mott said sweetly. "Enjoy your dinner, gentlemen. Good evening."

As Mott and her entourage left the dining room, Cuyler said, "Good Lord, Thad, why did you agree to that? Haven't we got enough work to do without humoring these women?"

"He's right," Cooper chimed in. "They'll take at least a half a day of our time."

"Ah, but it'll be worth it," Stevens soothed. "First of all, they'll make our clients more comfortable. And secondly, they'll help our case."

"How?" Cuyler asked suspiciously.

"You'll see," Stevens replied.

*e*ach day of the trial, the shackled prisoners sat in the same spot on a long bench directly behind the defense attorneys. And behind the prisoners, knitting away furiously, were Lucretia Mott and the other members of the Female Anti-Slavery Society.

As the proceedings wound down one Friday afternoon, the defense recalled Marshal Kline.

"Mr. Kline," defense attorney Cuyler began, "identify, if you will, some of those who were at Parker's the day of the shooting."

"Objection!" John Ashmead, the prosecutor, broke in. "We've been over this ground before."

"Proper identification is the heart of the case, your honor," Cuyler protested.

"Objection overruled," said Judge John J. Kane.

"Well," Kline said, after being asked to proceed, "there were those we ain't caught yet. And then there was Gorsuch's slaves."

"Name one," Cuyler urged.

"Noah Buley."

"And where is he sitting?"

"Third from the left," Kline said, pointing at the prisoner's bench.

"Name some others."

"James Buford, Clem Jones, Samuel Brown. And—"

"That's enough," Cuyler said. "Now, tell us where they are seated in the order you just stated."

Kline looked puzzled, but went on, "Fourth from the right, uh, sixth from the right, and, uh, uh, second from the left!"

"Thank you, Mr. Kline. No further questions."

With that, court was adjourned for the day.

*t*he next day, a Saturday, there was to be a morning session starting at 9 A.M.

But at 9:10, with Judge Kane, the jury, attorneys, and spectators seated, the prisoner's bench was still empty.

"Where are the prisoners?" the judge asked impatiently.

"Coming, Your Honor," a bailiff replied, trying to hide a smile.

When the prisoners finally appeared and shuffled to their bench, gasps of astonishment burst from every corner of the courtroom.

The prisoners, smiling broadly, were dressed in identical—and obviously new—gray suits. All were cleanly shaved and barbered. And each wore a red, white, and blue wool scarf around his neck.

"Order!" called the judge, repeatedly banging away with his gavel. "Order! Order!"

The Female Anti-Slavery Society needed no such admonition. During the furor, they kept their heads bent over their knitting.

As the proceedings began, Theodore Cuyler rose and said, "Your Honor, I would like again to call Marshal Kline."

Ashmead was on his feet immediately. "If it's for the purpose of further identification, I object!" he said.

"On what grounds?" the judge asked.

"On grounds that it's repetitive and the defense has set out to entrap my witness!"

"Asking a witness to identify the accused is hardly entrapment," Cuyler interjected dryly.

"I agree," said the judge. "Proceed, Mr. Cuyler."

With Kline back on the stand, Cuyler said. "Yesterday, you named Noah Buley, James Buford, Clem Jones, and Samuel Brown as being at Parker's. Is that correct?"

"Yes," Kline replied, his brow now moist with sweat.

"And yesterday, you very easily pointed out where they sat. Could you do that again?"

"Objection!" Ashmead said.

"Overruled."

Kline took a deep breath. "Well, uh, Buley's third from the left. And, uh, Buford is fourth from the right. Jones sixth from the right and Samuel Brown, uh, second from the left."

"Will each of those named please stand up," Cuyler asked, looking at the prisoners.

As the prisoners rose, there was another outburst in the courtroom. None was in the position indicated by Kline.

"Order!" said the judge, again banging his gavel.

Ashmead rose to his feet. "This is highly irregular, if not unethical, Your Honor," he said. "Counsel for the defense is making a sham and mockery of this case with his theatricals."

"We have done nothing more than change the seating order of the prisoners, Your Honor," Cuyler said. "Mr. Kline, given the names by Harvey Scott, memorized where each defendant sat. And since the defendants sat in the same place every day, he was able to easily make identification.

"He doesn't know these unfortunate men. He can't say positively that they were at Parker's that fateful day."

"But the clothes, your Honor!" Ashmead said. "Counsel for the defense set out to deliberately confuse Mr. Kline."

"Your Honor, the clothes were made and donated by a group of compassionate ladies who reside in this city.

"With a very humane and industrious effort they took these poor individuals out of the rags they were arrested in and were kind enough to dress them decently in this cold weather.

"If anything, these wonderful ladies should be applauded and given a vote of thanks for their generosity and concern for these unfortunate men."

The courtroom now rang with applause, cheers, boos, and catcalls.

Through it all, the Female Anti-Slavery Society knitted on.

*h*aving completed their attack on Kline, the defense now began to concentrate on Harvey Scott.

One of the witnesses called was Edward Carr, a blacksmith. Carr said Scott was an apprentice and had a room in the attic of his house. To get to the attic, Scott had to go through a room where his granddaughters slept, and climb a set of stairs.

Thaddeus Stevens took over for the defense. "Now, Mr. Carr," he said, "as I understand it, you locked Scott into the attic room every night out of concern for your granddaughters, is that right?"

"That's right."

"Would you tell us, then, what happened the night of September tenth?"

"I knew him to go up the stairs into my garret on the night of the tenth between eight and nine o'clock. I buttoned the door after he went up, on the outside from the stairs in the room, where the stairs started. I knew nothing more about him until a quarter of an hour before sun-up when I unbuttoned the door and called him to come down. He answered and came down directly, then made a fire in my house.

"Immediately after he had the fire going, he went for a cow in a two-acre lot. He brought her down between my garden and shop where we generally milk her. He went into the shop and went to work. He worked till breakfast time and we had our breakfast, and he went back with me into the shop and was not out of my employ for the rest of the day, the eleventh."

"No further questions at this time, Your Honor," Stevens said.

The prosecution began to cross-examine Carr.

"How far is your house from Parker's?" John Ashmead asked.

"I would suppose about three miles."

"Is there a window in the attic room where Harvey Scott slept?" Ashmead went on.

"Yes."

"Could he have gotten out of that window?"

"Yes. But he would have to drop down about ten feet to the roof of a shed and then from the shed to the ground. And if he did go out the window, he couldn't get back."

"Nothing further," Ashmead said wearily.

Still, Harvey Scott stuck to his story. He said he was at Parker's and identified Henry Simms, one of the defendants, as the man who shot Gorsuch. He also identified other defendants in the dock, saying they were at Parker's.

But on December fourth, after the defense said it had no further testimony to offer, the prosecution decided to recall Harvey Scott in the rebuttal phase of the case.

The prosecution knew that Edward Carr's testimony was very damaging. It wanted Scott to again refute that testimony.

But the prosecution was in for a surprise.

*t*he prosecution wasted no time the following morning. "Harvey Scott to the stand, please."

As soon as Scott settled in his chair, John Ashmead went right to the heart of the matter.

"Were you at Parker's the morning of the eleventh of September last?" Ashmead asked.

Scott took a moment, then, with downcast eyes, said, "I was proved to be there, but was not there."

Ashmead was stunned. Thinking he had misunderstood the witness, he repeated the question: "On the morning of the eleventh of September?"

"No, sir," Scott said, raising his head and looking Ashmead in the eye. "Kline swore I was there, and at the time I was taken up, I told the man I was not there, and they took me to Christiana, and I was frightened, and I didn't know what to say, and I said what they told me."

Ashmead, obviously upset, looked at the judge, "I had a conversation with this witness three or four days ago, Your Honor, and he said he was there."

Turning to Scott, Ashmead said, "Do you understand my question when I ask you whether, on the morning of the eleventh of September last, at Parker's house, you were present?"

"That was what I said before."

"Do you say so now?" the judge broke in.

"No, sir." Harvey Scott answered.

Soon after Harvey Scott recanted, the defense and the prosecution made final summations of their

Castner Hanway, who became a Quaker after the trial, was considered a hero and was made an honorary member of every Masonic lodge in Pennsylvania. Here he is pictured with his wife, Martha, and their son, Robert.

cases and the judge charged the jury. The jury left the courtroom and returned fifteen minutes later.

"Gentlemen of the jury, have you agreed upon your verdict?" the clerk of the court asked.

In unison, the jury replied, "Yes, sir!"

Turning to Castner Hanway, the clerk said, "Prisoner, stand up. Jurors, look upon the prisoner. Prisoner, look upon the jurors. How say you, jurors: Is Castner Hanway guilty of the treason of which heretofore he stands indicted, or not guilty?"

In one voice, the jurors answered, "Not guilty!"

With the case against Hanway so thoroughly demolished, charges against the remaining defendants were promptly dropped.

Less than a month later, a Lancaster County jury rendered another "not guilty" verdict against the defendants, this one in response to the murder charge and related offenses.

*A*fter the battle on September 11, Abraham Johnson, the Parkers, and the Pinckneys rushed away from the scene together.

The children were still in the care of Eliza's mother in the village, but Eliza and Hannah went into hiding at another location.

Leaving the women, Parker, Johnson, and Alexander Pinckney immediately went to the home of Marsh Chamberlain.

"Marsh, what do you think we ought to do?" Parker asked as they gathered in the Chamberlain barn, out of sight of passersby.

"You could give up, or your could run for Canada," Chamberlain said, his weathered face serious.

"Can't we just hide until this blows over?" Johnson asked.

"They'll find you," Chamberlain replied.

"And if they find us, they'll hang us," Pinckney said.

"Could be," Chamberlain responded.

"They'll never hang me," Parker responded.

Pinckney, who knew what Parker meant, said, "Me, either."

"Same here," Johnson added.

Pleased, Parker said, "Let's go back to my house and get some food and extra clothes."

On leaving Chamberlain's, however, they met two women on the road. "Parker!" one of them said. "Where are you going?"

"To my house, why?"

"Don't!" the second woman cried fearfully. "There are fifty men looking for you! And they all got guns!"

Realizing the extreme peril of the situation, Parker and his companions rejoined Eliza and Hannah for the rest of the day. After a long discussion, they decided there was only one safe course of action:

The men would strike out for Canada immediately. If they made it across the border, the two wives and the children would join them.

"I hate to do this," Parker said as he held Eliza when they were alone for a few moments.

"I know," Eliza said, kissing and hugging him. "But we have no other choice. And don't worry, we'll be all right."

Long after dark, Pinckney and Parker said good-bye to their families. With Johnson, they hurried to Levi Pownall's, hoping to get a supply of food for their trip north. Nearing the house, they came to a small, wooded area.

"You wait here," Parker said to Johnson. "We'll be back quick as we can."

When Parker and Pinckney arrived at the back door of the big farmhouse, they found Pownall's daughters, Elizabeth and Ellen, in the kitchen, washing dishes by candlelight.

Parker knocked lightly. Looking up from her task and recognizing Parker, Elizabeth quickly signaled "Quiet!" and snuffed out the candles.

Cautioning the men not to speak, the girls led them silently up a back staircase to the rooms above.

Only then did Parker learn that the Pownalls had a guest lying on a bed in the living room: the wounded Dickinson Gorsuch (who later recovered).

Worse yet, he was told that several of Gorsuch's friends from Maryland, along with half a dozen of Kline's deputies, were in and around the house to guard against a possible attack by the "rioters."

Just as Parker was worrying about how he could escape from the dangerous situation he had so innocently walked into, Sarah Pownall came up the stairs to take charge.

"You girls get two pillowcases, take them downstairs and fill them with food," she commanded in crisp, low tones. "And tell George and his brother I want them."

In thirty minutes, Sarah's youngest son, tow-headed George Pownall, who was eighteen, slipped out of the back door and placed the pillowcases under "the Queen apple tree."

In that same thirty-minute period, Levi Jr., his older brother and the tallest member of the family, quietly brought several items of clothing from various closets.

Shortly thereafter, Parker and Pinckney, wearing typical gray Quaker clothes, including broad-brimmed beaver hats and large overcoats, walked out of the house, each with a Pownall daughter on his arm.

No one paid any attention to the "gentlemen callers" as they boldly left the house and bowed a polite "good night" to Ellen and Elizabeth at the front gate.

*C*arrying the pillowcases filled with food, Parker and Pinckney rejoined Johnson and headed north for a station they knew to be on the Underground Railroad.

Two women, Elizabeth Coates and Ann Preston, both Quakers, rushed them to a farm owned by Isaac and Dinah Mendenhall, both of whom were opposed to the "accursed" Fugitive Slave Act. After

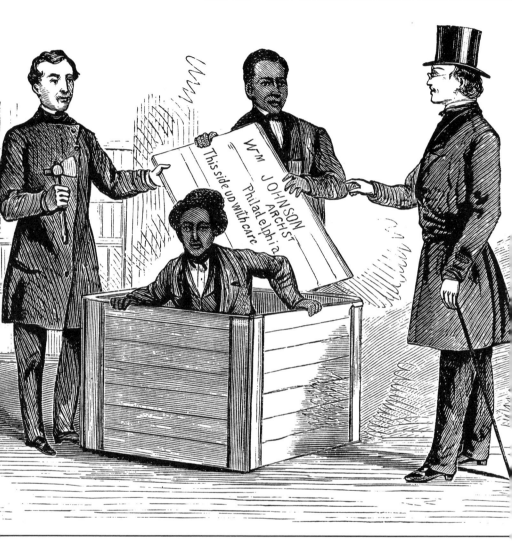

*Abolitionists resorted to all sorts of tricks
to help blacks escape from slavery.*

a night in the Mendenhall barn, Dinah Mendenhall put them in a wagon, covered them with hay and delivered them to the home of three Quaker sisters.

"These are the times that try men's souls, and women's too," Mrs. Mendenhall laughed as she said good-bye to her cargo.

After spending a night in the barn of the three Quaker sisters, Parker and his friends moved steadily northward. Sometimes they were on horseback, in canoes, or in the bottom of wagons. Often, they walked.

On reaching Norristown, they were hidden in the basement of a carpenter shop filled with wood shavings. The town was being watched by a large contingent of police.

After dark, one of Parker's benefactors came to their hiding place.

"We've got to get you away, there's too many police nosing around," he whispered.

"Good, but how?" Parker asked.

"Oh, we got a plan. Let's hope it works."

Here was the plan: By midnight, five wagons would be assembled outside the carpenter shop. Each would leave at a different time and go in a different direction. Only the last wagon would carry the fleeing blacks.

The decoys worked. Several days later in upstate New York, Parker and the others boarded a train that was to take them to Rochester, and the home of Frederick Douglass.

But the train trip was not without its scary and astonishing moments.

On boarding the train, Parker took a seat next to a jovial white man who appeared to be a traveling salesman. Pinckney and Johnson seated themselves nearby.

"I'm Christopher Larkin," the man said, extending a hand. "Nice to meet you," Parker responded. Just as he was about to give his name, a newsboy passed through the lone passenger car, crying, "Extra! Extra! Blacks murder whites!"

Larkin and several other passengers eagerly bought the paper and turned to the account of the Christiana "riot."

"Look at this," Larkin said. "A statesman killed and his son and nephew badly wounded."

"How horrible," Parker said. "And where was this?"

"Christiana," Larkin said.

"Never heard of it."

"It's near Philadelphia."

"Uh-huh," was Parker's only response.

Now, others began to comment on the Christiana story.

"Two thousand reward for this Parker!"

"That's a lot of money!"

"I'd collar him for that," one man said.

"And get yourself killed," his wife said sourly. "You've got a family, you know."

"Oh, I know, I know," the man said, rolling his eyes in mock pain.

As the train moved, Larkin said, "This Parker must be a powerful man."

"Really?" Parker asked.

"Says here the whites were scared to death of him."

"That's interesting."

Just then, Johnson called Parker from his seat and led him to the rear platform of the car. "We got to get off this damned train!" he said.

"Why?" Parker asked.

"Why? Because they're gonna find out who we are."

"Until they do, I ain't movin'," Parker said and returned to his seat.

"What do you think will happen to this Parker if they catch him," Parker asked Larkin.

"If he was tried in Maryland, they'd hang him," Larkin said. "But not in Pennsylvania. But they won't get Parker, he's in Canada by now. At least, I hope so. You colored people should look at Parker the way we would look at our brave men."

"How do you mean?" Parker asked.

"Well, don't you see?" Larkin explained. "He wasn't fighting for glory. Or for praise. He was fighting for liberty. You should protect him and remember him as long as you live."

When they left the train at Rochester, Larkin again shook hands with Parker. "It was nice traveling with you," he said. "I'd like to do it again sometime."

Not once during the journey did Larkin ask for Parker's name.

*f*rederick Douglass was well known in Rochester, and the fugitives had little trouble finding his house.

"I've been expecting you," Douglass said on opening the door to the trio. "Quick, come in."

As soon as the weary travelers were comfortable, Douglass told them they couldn't stay long.

"You must remember, you are not only fugitives from slavery, you have been charged with murder," he said quietly. "The news about the fight, with your descriptions, has already been telegraphed to police all over the country."

"We guessed that," Parker responded.

"Fortunately," Douglass said, "the search, according to the papers, is being concentrated in the mountains to the east. Don't ask me why. In any event, you can't tarry here too long."

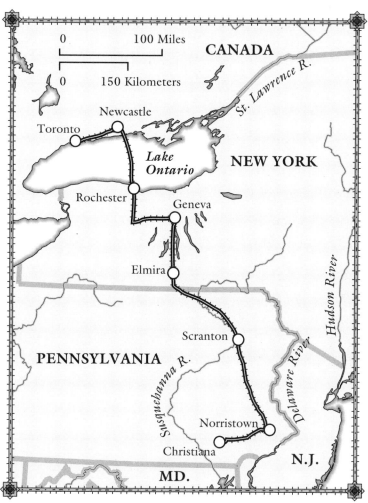

With the help of the Underground Railroad, Parker fled
Christiana. At some point, he "took the [railroad] cars."
In the 1850s, continuous rail service was not available,
and it was necessary to switch from one railway line to
another. If Parker boarded a train in Pennsylvania, he
would have had to change trains five or six times during
his twelve-day journey to Rochester, New York.

Douglass said he would have some of his friends check the crossing points to Canada to see if any were unguarded.

"You can be sure the main crossings will be watched twenty-four hours a day," he said. "So you are in a dangerous and critical situation even though you're a long way from Christiana."

After dark the next day, Douglass gave the men a fast ride in his carriage to a landing on the Genessee River and put them aboard a steamer just minutes before it was scheduled to sail for Canada.

Parker and his friends went to the deck rail to wave good-bye to Douglass, who was standing on the pier below. As the bell rang for the gangplank to be raised, two policemen appeared next to Douglass.

"Bon voyage, William Parker!" Douglass called mockingly.

The startled policemen looked up as Parker waved and bellowed with a hearty laugh, "Be sure to tell Kline I'm in Canada!"

*A*lthough all arrived safely in Canada, Parker learned from an Underground Railroad agent they met in Toronto that he was not yet out of danger.

"Pennsylvania has asked Canadian authorities to take you and your friends into custody and return you for trial," the agent said. "If you can be found, of course."

"Let's get out of here!" Pinckney said.

"I agree," Johnson said. "We get out of the city and into the woods and they'll never find us."

"You go if you want to," Parker said. "I want to think a little before I go running off to starve in the wilderness and freeze to death."

After talking things over with the agent, Parker decided to go to the Government House and find out whether or not the Canadians would regard him as a free man.

"I'm William Parker," he said to the first person he met in Government House. "Somebody said the Governor of Pennsylvania wants me sent back and I came to see what could be done about it."

Very soon, he was ushered into a large office where he was greeted by a small, round man with a bald head.

"So you're William Parker?" the man said as they shook hands.

"That's me," Parker said.

"I'm Jim Williams. Have a seat and let's talk."

Seating himself opposite Parker on the other side of the desk, Williams took out a folder, wrote on the face of it, set it aside, then took out a pad of paper.

After a few questions about his trip, Williams told Parker that Pennsylvania had, indeed, asked for his extradition under a treaty the United States had with Canada.

"Will you go?" Williams asked.

"I ran away from my master to be free," Parker said. "I ran away from the United States to be free. I'm done running."

Williams smiled. "Sounds like the answer is no."

"That's the answer," Parker said in a tight, low voice as he watched Williams make notations.

"Are you a fugitive from labor?" Williams asked.

"I am."

"What was your master's name?"

"David McCullough Brogden."

"Where does your master live?"

"Anne Arundel County, Maryland."

"Where is that?"

"Near Baltimore."

"Does the farm where you lived have a name?"

"Nearo," Parker said.

"Do you have a family?"

"Yes."

"Will they be joining you?"

"I pray to God they will!" Parker answered.

Williams had several more questions. Then he said, "Will you swear that all of the answers you have given me are truthful?"

"Yes," Parker said.

"Sign here," Williams said, pushing the paper in front of Parker.

"I can't write," Parker said stiffly.

"Well, then, make some kind of mark, or a picture."

Parker took Williams's pen and after some thought carefully drew two small hearts near the "x" at the bottom of the page.

Williams studied the signature, shook his head, opened the folder, put the paper inside and closed it. Parker, who was watching every move, said in a deep, still voice, "Well, are you going to try to send me back or not?"

Williams looked at Parker for a moment, then got up from his desk and walked around it. When he was face-to-face with the big black man, he thrust out his hand.

"Your family can join you whenever you can arrange it," he said.

Parker, experiencing a sudden burning sensation behind the eyes, blinked rapidly, not sure he had heard right. "Does that mean—?"

"It means, William Parker, that you are now as free as I am."

*t*o Parker, freedom would not be what it ought to be without Eliza and the children. Luckily, with the aid of the Underground Railroad, the family was re-united within a few months.

THE

ATLANTIC MONTHLY.

A MAGAZINE OF

Literature, Science, Art, and Politics.

VOLUME XVII.

BOSTON:
TICKNOR AND FIELDS,
124 TREMONT STREET.

LONDON: TRÜBNER AND COMPANY.
1866.

Parker's autobiography was published in Atlantic Monthly *magazine in 1866, only a year after the Civil War ended. Interestingly, the editor notes that the Christiana Riot, ". . . more than any other event, except the raid of John Brown, helped to precipitate the two sections [of the country] into the mighty conflict which has just been decided on the battlefield."*

From Toronto the Parkers made their way westward to a colony for black immigrants in Buxton, a village in Raleigh Township, Ontario. The colony was founded by Dr. William King, a Presbyterian minister determined to prove that former slaves could become productive citizens.

Like others who settled in the self-governed colony, Parker bought a fifty-acre lot, agreeing to pay for it at the rate of twelve dollars and fifty cents a month over a ten-year period.

Parker also went to adult night school where he learned to read and write. Soon he became a correspondent for Frederick Douglass's publication, *North Star.* He was also elected (and re-elected many times) to the Raleigh Township Council by voters who were both black and white.

Parker wrote an autobiography titled *The Freedman,* at about the time of the Civil War. Sometime after it was completed, friends sent it to *Atlantic Monthly* magazine with the suggestion that the editor "revise it for publication or weave its facts into a story which would show the fitness of the Southern black for the exercise of the right of suffrage."

The editor said, however, that the manuscript required no revision. It was written ". . . in a clear legible hand; its words are correctly spelled; its facts clearly stated and—in most instances—its sentences are properly constructed."

"On reading it over carefully," the editor added, "I also discover that it is in itself a stronger argument for the manhood of the negro than any which could be adduced by one not himself a free man, for it is the argument of facts and facts are the most powerful logic."

Parker's story was published in two installments in the magazine in 1866.

But even without the magazine story, those who lived in the Christiana area remembered Parker and his family.

Lindley Coates, a Quaker farmer who knew Parker, found him to be "bold as a lion, the kindest of men, and the most steadfast of friends."

Another Quaker farmer, Moses Whitson, said that Parker was ". . . possessed of resolution, courage and action" and that he could ". . . work hard all day, and walk ten to fifteen miles at night to organize his people."

Years later, Thomas Whitson (Moses Whitson's son), who also had known Parker, spoke of him at ceremonies commemorating the battle at Christiana.

Whitson said the real significance of Parker's stand was this:

". . . In all the slave hunting era, during all the period of mob violence attending the anti-slavery struggle up to that time, there had been no open resistance to the authority of the Government.

Forty-five years after the trial, defendants Samuel Hopkins and Peter Woods visit the crumbling remains of what is still known as the Riot House. In their teens at the time of the riot, both were working in the fields when arrested. The corn cutter in Hopkins's hand was the only weapon carried by the majority of those who answered Eliza Parker's call for help. This photograph is the only one known to exist of any of the black defendants.

"This man advanced out in his yard, struck the United States down in open battle in the person of Gorsuch. It was this that caused the matter to be published in every paper in the land, to be noticed even in England and made the entire slave empire tremble from the Potomac to the Rio Grande.

"It was not because Gorsuch was killed, or that his son and nephew were badly wounded, that this community was scoured for weeks by bandits disguised as United States Marshals, or that Marines were sent . . . but because one brave man, preferring death to slavery, said, 'I don't care for you or the United States, there will be no slaves taken back from here while I am alive'!"

There is also this to remember:

William Parker, the Christiana rebel, took a stand that showed America that the Compromise of 1850, hinged as it was to the injustice of the Fugitive Slave Act and the infamy of slavery itself, could not hold the nation together for very long.

It demonstrated, in other words, that the Compromise was really not a compromise, but a grudging agreement to delay the inevitable.

Parker's defiance of the Fugitive Slave Act was also an important milestone in a continuing struggle for what many take for granted and others—in America and elsewhere—still seek: freedom of the mind, the spirit, and the body.

~ *epilogue* ~

In the prelude to the Civil War there were many incidents and events that added fuel to the raging fire of
rhetoric and emotion that swept the country. But
none were so volatile and none so fiercely shaped
opinions as the Christiana Riot in 1851, the Supreme
Court's Dred Scott decision in 1857, and John
Brown's raid on Harper's Ferry on 1859.

In Dred Scott, a principle finding held that since
Scott was a Negro he could not be a citizen of the
United States; and since he was not a citizen he could
not sue for his freedom from slavery. It added that
slavery could (under certain conditions) exist legally
anywhere in the country.

John Brown's raid, on the other hand, was part of a white zealot's plan to build an army of whites and blacks to somehow attack the South and liberate the slaves.

In terms of historical significance, these three events can be compared to the Sons of Liberty uprisings against the Stamp Act, the burning of the British Royal Navy Cutter *Gaspee,* and the Boston Tea Party—inflammatory incidents that planted the seeds of the American Revolution.

But it was the Christiana Riot—a single, little-known episode in American history—that lit the fuse that ultimately exploded into Civil War. Christiana said to those who would listen that the compromise would ultimately be breached. Christiana said further that the slavery question—as Clay, Webster, and others predicted—could never be settled without bloodshed.

In an eloquent and historic speech, given only seven years after Christiana, Abraham Lincoln put it this way:

"A house divided against itself cannot stand.

"I believe this government cannot endure, permanently half slave and half free. I do not expect the Union to be dissolved—I do not expect the house to fall—but I do expect it will cease to be divided.

"It will become all one thing, or all the other."

∧∧∧

John Rosenburg spent ten years in the New York bureau of United Press International as a general correspondent, feature writer, sportswriter, and columnist. He is also the author of *The Story of Baseball* and several other books and magazine articles. Now retired from AT&T and Pennsylvania Bell, Mr. Rosenburg lives with his wife in a suburb of Philadelphia, just thirty-five miles from Christiana. He is currently at work on his next historical novel.